The Making of an Urban Community College in a Union and Political
Environment: An Historical Perspective of Wayne County Community College
District, Detroit, Michigan 1964-2016

By Dr. Willie J. Greer Kimmons
President, Wayne County Community College Downtown
Campus, Detroit, Michigan 1979-1983

authorHOUSE®

AuthorHouse™
1663 Liberty Drive
Bloomington, IN 47403
www.authorhouse.com
Phone: 1 (800) 839-8640

Published by AuthorHouse   09/21/2016

ISBN: 978-1-5049-7142-3 (sc)
ISBN: 978-1-5049-7141-6 (e)

Print information available on the last page.

Any people depicted in stock imagery provided by Thinkstock are models,
and such images are being used for illustrative purposes only.
Certain stock imagery © Thinkstock.

This book is printed on acid-free paper.

Because of the dynamic nature of the Internet, any web addresses or
links contained in this book may have changed since publication and may
no longer be valid. The views expressed in this work are solely those
of the author and do not necessarily reflect the views of the publisher,
and the publisher hereby disclaims any responsibility for them.

Pictures of the Central Administration Building, the five major campuses and their addresses.

District Office
801 W Fort
Detroit, Michigan 48226
313-496-2600

Downriver Campus
21000 Northline Road
Taylor, Michigan 48180
734-946-3500

Downtown Campus
1001 W. Fort St.
Detroit, Michigan 48226
313-496-2758

Eastern Campus
5901 Conner
Detroit, Michigan
313-922-3311

Northwest Campus
8551 Greenfield road
Detroit, Michigan 48228
313-943-4000

Western Campus
9555 Haggerty Road
Belleville, Michigan 48111
734-699-7008

District Office
801 W Fort
Detroit, Michigan 48226
313-496-2600

Downriver Campus
21000 Northline Road
Taylor, Michigan 48180
734-946-3500

Downtown Campus
1001 W. Fort St.
Detroit, Michigan 48226
313-496-2758

Eastern Campus
5901 Conner
Detroit, Michigan
313-922-3311

Northwest Campus
8551 Greenfield road
Detroit, Michigan 48228
313-943-4000

Western Campus
9555 Haggerty Road
Belleville, Michigan 48111
734-699-7008

Table of Contents

DEDICATION

This historical perspective is dedicated to the many visionary and brave men and women who fought in the trenches to bring Wayne County Community College into fruition. They improved the lives of children, youth and families through education in the great city of Detroit and the county of Wayne. These men and women were the foot soldiers that made the ultimate sacrifice. The 1964 Citizens Advisory Council (CAC), along with the 1967 riots, helped create the Wayne County Community College concept.

When I think of the struggles and sacrifices that many concerned citizens made to birth Wayne County Community College into a reality, I am often reminded of the saying of the late, great Fredrick Douglass: "If there is no struggle, there is no progress. Those who profess to favor freedom, and yet deprecate agitation, are men who want crops without plowing up the ground. They want rain without thunder and lightning. They want the ocean without the awful roar of its many waters. This struggle may be a moral one; or it may be a physical one; or it may be moral and physical; but it must be a struggle. Power concedes nothing without a demand. It never did and never will..."

Frederick Douglass
Abolitionist

ACKNOWLEDGEMENTS

The statements contained in this book represent the observations, evaluations and personal interviews of current and past members of the Board of Trustees, representatives from the state legislature, civic organizations, current and former administrators, staff, faculty and students at Wayne County Community College (WC3) in Detroit, Michigan. In addition, a series of publications and documents reflecting the history of Wayne County Community College that were provided by the institution proved to be invaluable resources.

Special appreciation and thanks to Dr. George Boggs, Former President and CEO of The American Association of Community Colleges (AACC), Washington, D.C.; and the following Wayne County Community College personnel: Trustee Juanita C. Ford, Member of Wayne County Community College Board of Trustees, the longest, active serving member of the Board of Trustees; Dr. Curtis L. Ivery, Chancellor of Wayne County Community College District, Detroit, Michigan; Mrs. Martha J. Grier, Assistant to the Chancellor for Board and Public Relations; Dr. Jacqueline Hodges, Former Campus President, Downtown Campus; Mrs. Amanda Davis, former Director of Student Services; Dr. Arthur Carter, former President of the Northwest Campus; Dr. Rafael Cortada, former President of Wayne County Community College District; Dr. Thomas F. Waters, former President of Wayne County Community College District; Dr. Thelma Vriend, former Vice President for Student Services, Wayne County Community College District; Mr. Sammie Rice, Chief Operational Officer for Facilities and former President of the UAW; Mr. Thomas Howard, Jr., former Chief Operational Officer for Finance and Administration and former Director of Purchasing; Dr. Ronald Temple, former President, Wayne County Community College District; Dr. Reginald Wilson, former President, Wayne County Community College District; and many, many others for their tireless efforts, collaboration and invaluable support in the completion of this historical perspective of Wayne County Community College in Detroit, Michigan. Thanks to the many writers who granted permission to use their work and to the number of proof-readers and editors who read the numerous drafts of this worthwhile document.

It is a distinct honor and a personal privilege to recognize the major educational contributions that a number of students, staff, faculty, community leaders, concerned citizens, and political representatives have made in the development of Wayne County Community College. I am grateful for this opportunity to acknowledge professionally the significant role that Wayne County Community College has played in the lives of Black and White Americans and others, throughout Wayne County, the State of Michigan and the United States of America. The leadership, support and development of Wayne County Community College was the making of an historical proportion and the lifelong dream of many great citizens of Detroit, Michigan.

INTRODUCTION

As the former president of Wayne County Community College's Downtown Campus, 1979-1983, I was commissioned on September 28, 1982 by the Board of Trustees and former Interim President Dr. Thomas Walters to write the history of Wayne County Community College Detroit, Michigan, 1964-2016. After many, many years of research and interviews, the book is finally completed. Its title is the <u>Making of an Urban Community College in a Union and Political Environment: An Historical Perspective of Wayne County Community College District, Detroit, Michigan, 1964-2016</u>. In addition, Dr. George Boggs, former President and CEO of the American Association of Community Colleges (AACC) (2000-2010) graciously consented to write the foreword to this book.

The manuscript will carefully discuss the beginning and turbulent struggle of Wayne County Community College in the 60's; the middle years of growth and pain of the 70's; the crisis of the 80's that almost closed the college; and the growth in the 90's and its current status of productivity and stability. In addition, the book will address community and instructional leaders' roles, duties, responsibilities and styles. Their commitments and obligations in the teaching, learning and leadership development process will also be addressed. The document will demonstrate how to plan, develop your own leadership style and how to inspire leadership in others. This body of work is an outgrowth of many years of discussions between citizens of Detroit, former students, teachers, staff, political and community leaders, Board of Trustees and former presidents of Wayne County Community College, Detroit, Michigan, whom I owe a tremendous amount of admiration, respect and appreciation.

FOREWORD

By Dr. George Boggs

As a lifelong educator in higher education and President and CEO of the American Association of Community Colleges, I realize the importance of this historical documentation of Wayne County Community College of Detroit, Michigan. This historical perspective is a "must read" for all educators, students, concerned citizens, taxpayers, community college personnel and the committed believers in the state of Michigan, Wayne County, and the great city of Detroit. The unusual birth and development of Wayne County Community College is carefully illustrated and outlined in the book. The title, <u>The Making of An Urban Community College in A Union and Political Environment: A Historical Perspective of Wayne County Community College—1964-2016</u> is quite appropriate, fitting and timely for this special and unique educational institution.

The book cites many challenges and difficult circumstances that created and planted the seed to establish the Wayne County Community College District. Numerous challenges are described in the book from the Detroit riots of the 60's to the lack of support of a millage, to the growth of the automobile industry, to the "White Flight" from the city to the suburbs of Wayne County. As a result of these circumstances and many more, Wayne County Community College was created, formed, nurtured, and survived the past 52 years.

The book can be used as an educational resource for educators at all levels from public schools, two-and four-year colleges and universities, to churches, union groups, and political organizations, local and federal governmental agencies. It should be required reading for history, political science and education departments in the areas of: community college administration, educational leadership, supervision, curriculum and instruction, educational administration in higher education, counseling education, reading and introduction to education. This book serves as a resource of information on how to survive in an urban setting and be productive in a union and political environment as an educational institution. It serves as a constant reminder that if concerned citizens are focused, committed and persevere long enough, anything can be accomplished. As a result of these efforts, Wayne County Community College today is a viable, stable, and flag-ship community college district that can be admired by everyone. Many thanks to the supporters, political leaders, community leaders, board of trustee members, business leaders, teachers, staff and outstanding students. We look forward to great things from the Wayne County Community College District in the future as a leader in the teaching and learning process. I encourage all interested educators, business leaders, political leaders, students, community leaders and concerned citizens to read this book.

With warm regards,
Dr. George R. Boggs
Former President and CEO
American Association of Community Colleges
One DuPont Circle, NW Suite 410
Washington, DC 20036

A Historical Perspective of Wayne County Community College Detroit, Michigan (1964-2016)
A Historical Overview of the Two-Year College Movement in the United States
Dr. George R. Boggs

From relatively modest nineteenth century beginnings, community colleges in the US have grown to the point today that nearly half of all students in US higher education attend them. These institutions were established to provide every American with an opportunity to obtain up to two years of post-secondary education. Community colleges are regionally accredited institutions of higher education that offer the associate degree as their highest degree, although a few community colleges in some states have recently begun to offer a few selected baccalaureate degrees. The community college mission is to provide access, serve all segments of society, provide a comprehensive educational program, serve the community, focus on teaching and learning, and to foster lifelong learning.

In about 1835, private academies, the forerunners of American community colleges, began to appear in the US. These academies, with elements of both secondary and postsecondary curricula, offered a variety of courses that could transfer into a university curriculum, as well as vocational courses. Such institutions included two-year normal schools or teachers' colleges, as well as institutions for women and African Americans. While these institutions have either disappeared or changed to four-year status, they proved the value of higher education below the baccalaureate degree level.

By the latter part of the 19th century, some higher education leaders, influenced by the German system, argued that the first two years of collegiate education should be left to the secondary schools. This model freed universities from undergraduate education and allowed them to concentrate on the upper division, graduate, and professional curricula. In the view of these educators, some students from the "junior colleges," as they were beginning to be called, would transfer to the University for Additional Study, while others would end their education at grade 14. While this idea did not influence the structure of universities in the US beyond the University of Chicago, which created Junior College and Senior College divisions, it did stimulate the creation of the first community college.

In 1901, under the guidance of William Rainey Harper, the President of the University of Chicago, and J. Stanley Brown, the Principal of Joliet High School, Joliet Junior College was established near Chicago, Illinois. Most community college historians point to the founding of Joliet Junior College as the beginning of the Community College movement in America, a social movement that would open access to higher education and training opportunities to students who would not otherwise have had a chance doe to economic, mobility, and social barriers. Joliet is the oldest community college that is still in operation. Other areas of the US soon followed this model. In 1907, legislation approved in California allowed local school districts to offer the first two years of college work.

In 1917, the North Central Association of Schools and Colleges established specific standards for the accreditation of public and private junior colleges. Today, all of the community colleges in the US are accredited by one of the same six regional agencies that accredit four-year colleges and universities.

The coming of the Great Depression in the 1930s brought an unexpected boost to the Community College Movement. The pressures of economic hard times and the resulting high unemployment among all ages combined with the number of college-age youth led the states to establish sixty-five public junior colleges between 1933 and 1939. These institutions opened the doors for thousands of students at a cost they could afford and offered employment opportunities once they completed their studies.

A second significant growth period for community colleges began at the conclusion of World War II. Millions of returning veterans were eager to move back into the work force but they needed affordable education and training opportunities. The servicemen's Readjustment Act of 1944, commonly called the G. I. Bill of Rights, provided the financial aid that allowed hundreds of thousands of returning veterans to consider the possibility of higher education.

Out of concern for the capacity of the higher education sector to accommodate the enrollment demand caused by the G. I. Bill, President Harry Truman established a Commission on Higher Education in 1946. The Truman Commission report, issued in 1947, changed the course of higher education in the US from "merely being an instrument for producing an intellectual elite" to becoming "the means by which every citizen, youth, and adult, is enabled and encouraged" to pursue higher learning. The Commission's report marked the first general use of the term "community college" and recommended that they expand nationally to provide universal access to postsecondary education.

The greatest expansion of community colleges in the U.S. took place between 1960 and 1970. During that decade, more than 450 new community colleges opened their doors to accommodate education and training needs of the "Baby boom" generation (the children of the returning World War II soldiers). As a result, about 45% of all 18-year-olds, enrolled in a community college.

With the approval of the Higher Education Facilities Act of 1963 and the Higher Education Act of 1965, the U.S. federal government dramatically expanded its direct aid to community colleges and their students.

Through the Facilities Act, communities were given the means to construct new campuses and enlarge existing facilities. Through the Higher Education Act and its subsequent reauthorizations, the federal government provides a range of direct grants and loans to students based on financial need as a means of lessening the barrier of cost to higher education access.

While the early junior colleges focused on the transfer mission, that of providing students with the first two years of a baccalaureate education before moving to university, states in other parts of the US developed technical colleges to prepare students to enter the workforce. Over the years, these two types of institutions began to evolve into today's comprehensive community colleges. The technical colleges gradually began to offer transfer courses, and the junior colleges began to offer vocational courses. The colleges also began to offer a variety of remedial or developmental education courses to prepare students for college level work, community service courses to meet the needs of community members, and contract education courses to serve local industry. Depending upon location, these institutions may today be called community colleges, technical colleges, technical community colleges, or even junior colleges. However, no matter what they are named, these higher education institutions are commonly referred to as community colleges.

The birth and humble beginnings of Wayne County Community College in Detroit, Michigan was somewhat different than the two-year college movement in this country. However, the advent of the two-year college system was to include all segments of our community and to give them an opportunity to be educated at an affordable rate, regardless of race, creed, and color, social or economical barriers. We are proud of the accomplishments of the Wayne County Community College District and the many outstanding students they have trained for the field of work or through transfer options at a 4-year college or university. I am deeply honored to participate in writing the history of this great institution.

Dr. George R. Boggs
Former President and CEO
American Association of Community Colleges
One DuPont Circle, NW
Suite 410
Washington, DC 20036

ABOUT THE AUTHOR

Dr. Willie J. Greer Kimmons was born in Hernando, Mississippi. He was reared in Memphis, Tennessee. He attended public school and received his high school diploma from Frederick Douglass High School, Memphis, Tennessee. He was a student athlete and received an athletic scholarship to attend Lincoln University in Jefferson City, Missouri. While at Lincoln University, he was active in the Student Government Association and ROTC. Willie Kimmons served as a First Lieutenant in the United States Army, Adjutant General Corps, during the Vietnam era as an Administrative Data Processing and Personnel Officer.

Dr. Kimmons received his Bachelor of Science degree in Health Education and Psychology from Lincoln University in Jefferson City, Missouri. He received both a Master of Science degree in Curriculum and Instruction and a Doctorate degree in Education Administration and Supervision in Higher Education from Northern Illinois University in DeKalb, Illinois at the age of 28.

Dr. Kimmons served as President of the Downtown Campus of Wayne County Community College from 1979-1983. The Downtown Campus was the "showpiece" for the Wayne County Community College District serving more than 5,500 students in its first year of operation. He was the former vice President of Academic and Student Affairs, Lawson State Community College, Birmingham, Alabama and former interim President of Trenholm State Technical College in Montgomery, Alabama. Dr. Willie Kimmons was the founding Chancellor of Ivy Tech Community College in Bloomington, Indiana.

Dr. Kimmons has served at every level in the higher education teaching and learning process with dedication and distinction from classroom teacher, college professor, college dean, vice president, president and chancellor of two and four year colleges and universities. His interest in education stems from a background of training and experience in the area of human development, leadership, and community service. He is always eager to promote learning and development of the student by setting the atmosphere to motivate not only the student, but also individuals within the educational arena.

Dr. Willie Kimmons has spent his entire career getting to the root of understanding the nature of issues of today's parents, teachers and students. He has successfully dealt with many of the challenges of today's students throughout his career as a professional educator and community activist. His life's ambition is to expand enthusiasm for education and continue his commitment and dedication to the learner.

Dr. Kimmons' philosophy is... "that institutions should be committed to providing quality educational and health care services and should be held accountable by the communities they serve". He welcomes the challenge of giving and sharing leadership that supports these goals. He further believes that by uniting our energies and supporting our educational and health care systems, we will be able to keep our students academically challenged and our citizens better prepared for life. Dr. Willie J. Kimmons is the author of five books. His current two books are, <u>A Parenting Guidebook</u> for parents, grandparents, great-grandparents, schools, churches and communities to help save our children and save our schools. His godmother, the late, great, Honorable Shirley Chisholm former member of the US Congress, encouraged him to write the parenting guidebook. The second of the two current books is, <u>The Making of an Urban Community College in a Union and Political Environment: A Historical Perspective of Wayne County Community College District, Detroit, Michigan (1964-2016)</u>.

Dr. Kimmons' motto is ..."Help me to help somebody to save our children and save our schools; never, ever give up on our children, because our children are our greatest resource; our children are an extension of us; and our children are our future."

Currently, he is an educational consultant for PreK-16 Schools; Title I Schools, Teachers and Parents; an author and motivational speaker. He has given more than 500 presentations and lectures to a variety of organizations including educational associations; Chambers of Commerce; elementary, middle and high schools; 2-year colleges, 4-year colleges and universities; churches and other religious groups; Kiwanis; Rotary; Lions; NAACP; Urban League; economic development organizations; political groups; Greek organizations; youth groups; parenting groups; daycare centers; Head Start programs; civic and other community organizations.

Dr. Kimmons is "A Voice for Partners in Education". In 2005 he founded his corporation, "Save Children Save Schools, Inc.". It is an educational consultant service located at 1653 Lawrence Circle, Daytona Beach, Florida 32117; Office (386) 451-4780; Fax (386) 253-4920; E-mail address: wjkimmons@aol.com. His website is: www.savechildrensaveschools.com.

OPENING OF THE COLLEGE, THE EARLY YEARS 1964-1974

CHAPTER 1
COLLEGE HISTORICAL PERSPECTIVE

Wayne County Community College is a publicly supported two-year comprehensive community college. It was one of Michigan's 29 independent community college districts. The Wayne County Community District covers the Detroit metropolitan area and has three of its five campuses and the administrative offices located in Detroit. It served students in the Detroit metropolitan area, as well as the remainder of Wayne County, with the exception of the existing community college districts of Highland Park, Henry Ford, and Schoolcraft. In the beginning years, Wayne County was the fourth largest county in the United States with a service area encompassing approximately 500 square miles and a population of 2.4 million people.

During the fifties and early sixties, almost every metropolitan area developed a community college district to satisfy the educational needs of its citizenry. In 1964, a citizen's committee, formed by the Wayne County Intermediate School District, conducted a feasibility study to assess whether a community college was needed. A second objective was to determine what would be necessary to establish such an institution if the study suggested one was needed. Through the citizen's feasibility study of 1964, it was discovered that Wayne County was the largest metropolitan region in the United States without a coordinated community college system. The need for such a system was clearly affirmed.

In 1966, acting on the findings of the Citizens Advisory Committee study of 1964, the Michigan State Board of Education officially approved the establishment of the district. The college was developed within the framework of the State of Michigan's Community College Act of 1966. Section 389.105 of the act defines a community college and its educational programs.

An election was held on May 9, 1966 to put the question of a need for a community college in Wayne County to the voters. The citizens strongly supported the creation of a college and selected a board of trustees. Most importantly, the white citizens in the surrounding suburbs of Detroit rejected a supporting millage of 2.50 mills. Obviously, the college could not exist without funding. The suburban white citizens of Wayne County had serious reservations about supporting a community college for the county that would be located in the inner city of Detroit, which would serve a majority Black population. Therefore, the concept of having five major campuses strategically located throughout Wayne County was born.

In spite of additional efforts to develop citizen support to pass a millage in 1966, it became clear to college supporters that such a millage would not pass. Unfortunately, the citizens of Detroit and 35 other Michigan cities and townships were not to have the direct services of a community college system; for, it was again obvious that the college could not exist without adequate funding.

In many ways, the history of this college is unique. It reflects the struggle, pains, and triumphs of the urban community college movement across the United States. Ever since the college's inception, there have been conflicts, confrontations, struggles and turmoil. In spite of this, the educational delivery system has continued to operate and render services to its students and the citizens of Wayne County. Other educational institutions in this country would have succumbed to such political, economic, union and social pressures. This suggests that Wayne County Community College will not only survive, but will thrive in the coming years. Indeed, some people believe that Wayne County Community College (WCCC) is a valuable educational resource for Detroit and consider it unfortunate that the college apparently did not have the confidence of the community. In 1990, according to J. Weaver in a WJBK-TV news editorial, "this may be due in part to ineffective behavior on the part of

Wayne County Community College's Board of Trustees, such as decision-making that has led to negative publicity resulting in the defeat of an important millage. The College's image is a serious problem and public confidence is low."

CHAPTER II
LEGISLATIVE ACTION/CITIZENS ADVISORY COUNCIL (CAC)

In recognition of the millage reality for Wayne County Community College of Detroit, Michigan, on August 2, 1967, the Michigan State Legislature passed Senate Bill No. 630 (introduced by former State Senator Arthur Cartwright of Detroit) to create a community college district for Wayne County. On the same day, former Governor George Romney signed the bill into law. While it is impossible to determine exactly the precise reason for this unprecedented legislative action, initial supporters of the bill cite three explanations. They include: (1) the constant pressure on the state of Michigan from the 1964 Citizens Advisory Council (CAC) citing a need for a community college in the county of Wayne; (2) the occurrence of the 1967 Detroit riots, which emphasized serious racial, economic and educational disparity between Blacks and Whites, and fostered the need for immediate changes; (3) the presence of wide-spread political support for the establishment of a community college system within Wayne County; and (4) a feeling that the college could contribute to the economic vitality of the area; despite the fact that the citizens would not be directly involved in its financing. Whatever the specific reasons for its inception, the college had a unique creation.

Also unique was the fact that the new law provided for the development of seven trustee areas within the college district. Community college trustees are, usually, either elected or appointed at large and have responsibility for an entire college district. As it was with the other 28 community college districts, Wayne County's district was autonomous and its trustees were responsible only to the voters. The law also provided enabling language for the actual millage election. It set a maximum of three millage elections, within 24 months, if necessary. Finally, the legislature appropriated $150,000 to support academic planning and development of the new community college district. In addition, the first official operating budget of the College was based on a million dollar grant from the state of Michigan, as well as a $300,000 stipend from New Detroit Incorporated. New Detroit Incorporated was a diverse group of community leaders that was formed to stabilize the racial tension, economic development and educational concerns of the city of Detroit and the county of Wayne after the 1967 riots. Also, operational funds were anticipated from student tuition payments.

LEGISLATIVE ACTION IMPACTS WAYNE COUNTY COMMUNITY COLLEGE PROGRAMS AND SERVICES

THE VOTERS OF Wayne County defeated a second Wayne County Community College millage proposal in August of 1970. This defeat caused a severe financial crisis for the college. Despite high student enrollment, the number of instructional center were reduced.

The state government intervened and provided emergency funding that allowed the college to continue to operate. Next, the state legislature passed Public Act 139 of the Public Acts of 1971 (September 1971), and mandating that Wayne County Community College was given a tax rate from the school portion of county taxes of 0.18 mill for 1971-1972 and 0.25 mill in subsequent years.

The passage and signing into law of two bills; House Bills 4793 and 4787 in the 1973 session of the Michigan legislature had a decided effect on the future shape of Wayne County Community College. When Wayne County Community College was established by the Michigan legislature, the Wayne County Intermediate School District served as the "creating body" to establish the district lines of the service area. (House Bill 4793 transferred this responsibility to the College's Board of Trustees, which was in the process of planning its district reapportionment on the basis of the 1980 national census.

CONSTITUENT GROUP – CITIZEN'S ADVISORY COUNCIL (CAC)

The role of citizen participation in the development and history of Wayne County Community College is significant. The Citizen's Advisory Council for the College was created in 1964. In 1966, the Citizen's Participating Study Committee, a sub-committee of the Citizen's Advisory Council, published a county-wide report that assisted in the millage election of 1966. The Committee also played a role in the series of events that led to the legislative act that created the College in 1967.

Six months prior to the opening of the College, in the spring of 1969, Executive Director/Secretary Murray Jackson and the Board of Trustees engaged Professor Hartford Smith of Wayne State University to develop a citizen's involvement proposal. The proposal was drawn up and formally implemented with the appointment of former <u>Governor G. Mennen Williams</u> as the General Chairman of the first Area Citizen's Advisory Council (CAC) in the fall of 1969. On March 25, 1970, the first county-wide session of the CAC met.

The charge of the CAC was based upon the plan Professor Hartford Smith developed. His proposal was presented to the Board of Trustees on March 12, 1969. At that meeting the Trustees approved the plan in concept. The primary objectives of the CAC are:

1) The transmission of information about the College and its programs and purposes to all segments of the community;
2) The channeling of information from the community to the Trustees and staff of the College;
3) The formulation of recommendations—both formal and informal- regarding matters of policy and operation of the College; and
4) The fostering of community support for the College and its Students.

The citizen's committees consisted of three phases. The Area Citizen's Advisory Council (ACAC), one in each of the seven districts, was composed of citizens that provide a localized perspective to the educational needs of their subcommittees and daily operation of the College's instructional program. The Citizens Consultative Committee (CCC) consisted of people from major social, economic, civic and governmental institutions in the College's district. The CAC was an elected group from the seven-area Citizen's Advisory Committees and the Citizen's Consultative Committee. The CAC, representing local and general interests, directly communicated with the Board of Trustees since it periodically met jointly with the Board.

Governor Williams resigned from the CAC upon being elected to the Michigan Supreme Court in November 1970. Former Mayor Jerome P. Cavanaugh became the second Chairman of the CAC. During his tenure, the organizational structure of the CAC developed. The following subcommittees, which corresponded to the major functional areas of the College, were created and included: (1) Steering, (2) Academic Services, (3) Community Relations, (4) Program Planning Advisory and Facilities Development, (5) Finance and Management, (6) Personnel and (7) Student Services.

Attorney John K. Grylls was elected Chairman of the CAC in 1973. Chairman Grylls supported and assisted in the creation of the county-wide Steering Committee and the adoption of an extensive set of bylaws designed to improve the activities of the CAC units. Attorney Grylls resigned in September of 1074 to campaign for the Wayne County Community College Board of Trustee position from District One. His campaign was successful and he served as a Trustee for more than ten years. Next, Mrs. Erma Henderson, former Detroit City Council President, was elected General Chairwoman of the Citizen's Advisory Council (CAC).

CHAPTER III
THE FIRST BOARD OF TRUSTEES

The first Board of Trustees was elected on May 9, 1966 and consisted of a chairperson and five additional members. Each member represented the entire Wayne County area. The Board actually functioned as a "lay" board consisting of concerned citizens because it did not have a legitimate basis to conduct educational business. In order to be considered legitimate, three things needed to happen. They were: (1) creation of the district, (2) election of trustees and (3) passage of a millage. As mentioned previously, the citizens supported and voted for the development of Wayne County Community College, but not for a millage to support funding for the College. Nevertheless, the Board met three or four times as an ad hoc group from 1966-1968.

Subsequent to the action of the ad hoc Board, Wayne County Intermediate District Board of Education designated seven geographical trustee districts. Consequently, each of the original seven trustees, elected on June 10, 1968 represented a specific geographical area in Wayne County. This original Board of Trustees was still in office at the time of the first Wayne County Community College graduating class of 1970. The first Board of Trustees consisted of Chairperson Donald Thurber and members Horace Bradfield, Eugene Beauregard, Raymond Wojtowicz, Albert Finley, Roy Mix and John Ryan.

CHAPTER IV
THE FIRST DAY OF CLASSES and THE AQUISITION OF THE GARFIELD BUILDING

The Students Arrive

Symbolically, the first day of classes represents the physical birth of a college. The modest advertising campaign for Wayne County Community College told the residents of Wayne County that, finally, there was a college just for them. The Detroit Free Press advertisement called it a "People's" college. The Wayne County Community College Board of Trustees designed a fall 1969 course schedule for an estimated 2,000 applicants. However, 8,500 students came to register for the fall 1969 semester. Eight thousand and three hundred were full-time freshmen and two hundred were full –time sophomores. This remarkable turnout was due to: (1) convenient neighborhood locations, (2) an "open door" admissions policy, (3) low tuition fees and (4) successful planning of the College to meet the needs of the community. The phenomenal number of registrants required an immediate expansion of curricula, facilities, staff and faculty. In addition to full-time faculty and staff, five hundred and fifty-six part-time instructors and fifty-seven part-time counselors were employed.

Early Physical Facilities

Wayne County Community College began as an educational institution with no buildings or facilities of its own. It was the College that brought itself to the community and to the newly enfranchised student it served by holding classes in existing neighborhood buildings throughout the county.

To realize the dream of providing higher education to the citizens of Wayne County, the College ultimately established over 70 instructional facilities throughout Wayne County. For example, the support of area high schools was sought and

11

cooperative arrangements were entered into in order to provide teaching areas in twenty-two locations, in time for opening day in September 1969. In addition, the College leased surplus space in parochial schools to conduct day and evening classes. Finally, in September of 1969, 11,000 square feet of administrative office space was acquired on the fifth floor of an office building at 4612 Woodward Avenue, the Garfield Building in Detroit, Michigan.

CHAPTER V
CHIEF EXECUTIVE OFFICERS OF THE COLLEGE

For the purposes of this book, the title of Chief Executive Officer is interchangeable with other terms, such as, Executive Secretary/Director, President or Chancellor, used throughout this book to designate the Chief Executive Officer at the College. The following terms as defined by Willie J. Kimmons in <u>Black Administrators in Public Community Colleges: (Self-Perceived Role and Status,</u> (1977), are used to promote clarity in regard to their use in this book:

<u>Administrators</u> – those who are officially charged with the functions of administration. The educational administrator has been described as a generalist in education and a specialist in the process of administration.

<u>Administration</u> – is defined as a social process concerned with creating, maintaining, stimulating, controlling and formally unifying and organizing human beings to accomplish predetermined objectives. Administration refers to the performance of the administrative process by an individual or a group within the context of an organization in its environment.

<u>First- Level Administrators</u> – are those administrators who are functioning in the administrative capacity of chief administrator, chancellor or presidents of educational institutions.

<u>Second-Level Administrators</u> – are those administrators who are functioning in the administrative capacity of vice-president, dean or provost at their designated institutions.

<u>Third-Level Administrators</u> – refers to those administrators who are functioning in the administrative capacity of department chairperson, division chairperson, program coordinators and directors of programs of their designated educational institutions.

The above administrative terms are crucial for the reader's understanding of Wayne County Community College's different organizational structures from 1968 to 2016. The College went from a **single-controlled centralized** organizational structure to a **single-controlled multi-campus** comprehensive **decentralized** organizational structure. There were 5 regional-core instructional centers: (1) Downriver Center (2) Downtown Center (3) Greenfield Center (4) Western Center and (5) Eastern Center. Each center had a regional0core director/dean who reported to the divisional vice president for academic affairs located in the central office. Today, it is a multi-campus comprehensive decentralized organizational structure where the five campus directors/deans now carry the title of campus presidents. They make day to day decisions for his/her own campus and report directly to the chancellor in the central office.

The original structure of the College was a president and 5 regional directors/deans. Today, the College has a real decentralized, comprehensive community college district, with a chancellor, and five regional campus presidents. The authority and responsibility in this organizational structure lies in the hands of each regional campus president, not the central administrative office, as it did during the early years of the College. The administrative lines of demarcation are clearly defined today at Wayne County Community College. As a result, there is increased productivity, enhanced accountability and greater viability for the future.

Administrative leadership of Wayne County Community College has been quite fluid. The College has been able, nevertheless, to maintain its credibility and to provide leadership and educational opportunities for the citizens of Wayne County in spite of its turbulent history.

It is irrefutable that the Office of the President, Chancellor or Chief Executive Officer is viewed as unstable and negative given that eight of the 13 Chief Executive Officers of the College served during the ten-year period from 1980-1990.

This propensity for instability is highlighted in an editorial that appeared in the <u>Detroit News</u> (August 1990) suggesting that Wayne County Community College's rapid turnover of Chief Executive Officers accounted for much, if not all, of the problems related to mismanagement and wasteful spending that have characterized Wayne County Community College since it began in 1967. The editorial stated that, "Of thirteen Chief Executive Officers, at least four have been forced to leave". The College has had 13 Chief Executive Officers over a period of 48 years (1968-2016). The third Chief Executive Officer, Dr. Reginald Wilson served 9 of the 48 years, from 1971-1980. The thirteenth and current Chief Executive Officer, Dr. Curtis Ivery, has served for 21 of the 48 years. Dr. Ivery is the longest serving Chief Executive Officer in the history of Wayne County Community College to date, 1995-2016. Of the 13 Chief Executive Officers, two of them, Dr. Wilson and Dr. Ivery, have served 30 of the 48 years. In an attempt to resolve some of the management problems of Wayne County Community College, the Michigan legislature, in the mid-1980s, authorized the State School Superintendent to take control of Wayne State Community College until such time as it could stabilize its own management. Ten years later (1990), it was the sentiment that Michigan lawmakers might have to do something similar again, even to the point of questioning the need for Wayne County Community College, if drastic and immediate changes were not made.

Various college constituencies quickly learned that information and requests were probably more effective going directly to Board members rather than through regular channels. This further hampered the operation of the College because Board members have only a partial view and receive partial information. One of the greatest functions of any Chief Executive Officer is to gather all of the information and present balance and objective recommendations to the Board. This normal and productive process was totally disrupted by an ineffective and unstable Chief Executive Office.

Chief Executive Officer Succession at Wayne County Community College 1968-2016

The sequence of Chief Executive Officer's succession is as follows:

1. Mr. Murray Jackson was selected by the new Board of Trustees in August of 1968, to serve as Executive Secretary/Director of Wayne County Community College. He was granted a leave of absence from Wayne State College where he was Assistant Dean of Students for Urban Affairs. Mr. Jackson became Acting President in 1969 and President in 1970. He resigned in February, 1971.

2. Mr. Alfred M. Pelham, a retired public official, was appointed by the Board of Trustees as Interim President upon the resignation of Mr. Jackson. Mr. Pelham served until September of 1971.

3. After Mr. Pelham's resignation, Dr., Reginald Wilson, former Director of Black Studies at the University of Detroit, was appointed President by the Board of Trustees. He served from October of 1971 to May of 1980.

4. Upon the resignation of Dr. Wilson, Mr. William G, Herbert, former Vice-President for New Detroit, Inc., was appointed Interim President from June 1, 1980 to January 1981.

5. Mr. Richard Simmons, Jr., former Deputy Mayor of Detroit, became the fifth President of Wayne County Community College. He served from January 1981 to June 1982.

6. Dr. Thomas F. Waters, former Associate Vice-President for Instruction at Wayne County Community College, became Interim President in July 1982. His tenure as President lasted until February 1983.

7. In March 1983, the Board elected Mr. George Bell, former Director of the Detroit Child Abuse Center and former Chairman of the Wayne County Community

College Board of Trustees, was elected as President of Wayne County Community College. His tenure ended in December 1983.

8. In December 1983, the Board of Trustees voted again to oust another President of Wayne County Community College, Mr. George Bell, with a 4 to 3 vote.

9. The Board of Trustees reinstated Dr. Thomas F. Waters to be President, again, of Wayne County Community College, effective January 1984 to August 1985.

10. Dr. Ronald J Temple was selected President from September 1985 to September 1990. Dr. Temple was the Dean of University College at the University of Cincinnati in Ohio. He became the tenth President of Wayne County Community College and educational critics viewed his Presidency as the last hope for the College. In an article published in the July 16, 1986 issue of *The Chronicle of Higher Education* by N. Scott Vance, entitled, "Reformer Counts On 'Survival Atmosphere'", it states that the Presidency of Dr. Ronald J. Temple is viewed as Wayne County Community College's last chance at redemption.

11. From October 1, 1990 to June 1994, Dr. Rafael Cortada, former President of the University of the District of Columbia in Washington, D.D., became the eleventh President of Wayne County Community College in twenty-two years (1968-1990). According to a Detroit Free Press article, December 18, 1991, "Dr. Cortada's moves correct abuses, restores integrity by implementing sweeping changes that affect payroll and personnel". (Detroit Free Press, November 26, 1991)

12. Dr. Richard Turner, former President of Nashville Technical Community College, Nashville, Tennessee, became the Interim President of Wayne County Community College from July 1994 to October 1995.

13. Dr. Curtis L. Ivery became the first Chancellor of the new comprehensive Wayne County Community College District from October 1995 to the present. Dr. Curtis Ivery has revitalized the College image and its integrity.

His tenure as Chancellor has stabilized the College administratively, managerially and increased the overall morale of students, faculty, staff and community. Thus far, he is the longest tenured Chief Executive Officer in the history of Wayne County Community College. As a visionary leader, he has more than doubled the College's enrollment since assuming the role of Chancellor.

Chapter VI
MISSION OF THE COLLEGE

The mission of Wayne County Community College is a direct outgrowth of the Citizens' Participating Study Committee of the Citizen's Advisory Council of 1964. The mission of the College was developed within the framework of the Michigan Community College Act of 1966. Section 389.105 of the Act states the following about community colleges and programs:

1) A community college means an educational institution providing primarily for the persons above the twelfth grade age level and primarily for those within commuting distance, collegiate and non-collegiate level education, including area vocational-technical education programs which may result in the granting of diplomas and certificates including those known as associate degrees, but not including baccalaureate or higher degrees.

2) An area vocational-education program means a program of organized systematic instruction designed to prepare the following individuals for useful employment in recognized occupations:
   a) Persons who have completed or left high school and who are available for full-time study in preparation for entering the labor market.
   b) Persons who have already entered the labor market and who need training to achieve stability or advancement in employment.
   c) Persons enrolled in high school.

3. When programs or courses are provided for persons enrolled in high school, the provision of the programs or courses shall be requested for each of the individuals by the superintendent or his designated representative of the school district in which the person is enrolled.

4. The word 'area' in the phrase 'area vocational-technical education program' refers to the geographical territory

of the district, and whatever territory within the district as is designated as the service area of the district by the State Board of Education. A community college is eligible to receive such state aid and assistance as may be appropriated by the legislature for the aid and support of junior colleges or community colleges as stated in the Michigan Community College Act of 1966, Section 389.105.

In 1972, the mission statement was adopted by the Wayne County Community College Board of Trustees. It read as follows:

Wayne County Community College is an open-admission, two-year institution of higher education which provides career programs of one year and two years that yield certificates and two-year Associate Degrees, and that provide either transfer access to senior colleges or terminal career preparation. The instructional program of the College is offered in 26 facilities located strategically throughout Wayne County with the intention being to be easily accessible to every citizen in the area.

The College's mission has remained basically unchanged; however, studies have been conducted to increase the ability of the College to attain its stated mission and to ensure that the changing needs of the community are addressed by refinements in the institution's stated mission and, especially, in the continual updating of measurable goals. It is the objective of the College to realize the potential and to maximize the skills and intellectual attainment of every student who enrolls. To achieve this objective will require something that is quite different from the traditional, elitist structure of most institutions of higher education. Wayne County Community College will have to move in creative, innovative and risk-taking directions to meet the needs of the highly-diversified, multi-ethnic, and economically heterogeneous population which inhabits the Detroit metropolitan area. As part of that innovation, the College must:

a) Experiment with new educational and programmatic ideas;

b) Develop new assessment procedures for gauging student ability and progress;

c) Offer African=American and other ethnic studies for its substantial non-white population, as well as for the enlightenment of its white students;

d) Make effective, the decentralization of its facilities in the community;

e) Increase individualization of instruction through the use of application of new curriculum methods, new technologies, "school without walls" philosophy, etc.

f) Create new occupational roles and the appropriate training for them; and

g) Assist in encouraging community and student involvement in program development, institutional governance and decision-making, and in the evaluation of the College's progress toward attainment of its stated goals.

In keeping with Wayne County Community College's new mission as outline above, the College staff and Board of Trustees identified six basic goals as part of the College's Five-Year Master Facilities Study (1973-1978). These goals, many of which have been achieved, were to:

1) Construct or renovate five major regional core centers to be strategically located throughout the College's server district;

2) Purchase an adequate building adjacent parking, later to be renovated, to serve both the administrative and instructional needs of the College district;

3) Complete renovation of both the Park Avenue Building and the Woodward Annex/Garfield Building, and use them as specialized instructional centers with major emphasis devoted to computer instruction and services, as well as science and related allied health instructional programs;

4) Continue program planning aimed toward achieving a 50:50 ratio of career-to-career programs being devoted to vocational-technical programs; and college transfer programs;

5) Continue program planning in the direction of maintaining an equitable distribution of instructional programs, student services, and facilities within the proposed regional core centers throughout the service districts; and

6) Continue to maintain a close working relationship with the Citizen's Advisory Council, various K-12 districts, other colleges and universities, as well as related public and private community agencies that are concerned with adult and post-secondary education.

MIDDLE YEARS OF GROWTH
OF THE COLLEGE 1975-1995

CHAPTER VII
BAGAINING UNITS:

American Federation of Teachers, Local 2000 (AFT)
United Automobile Workers, Local 1796 (UAW); and
Professional and Administrative Association (P&AA).

Due to the impact of the automobile and related industries, unions in the state of Michigan played a key role in its economic, social and political arenas. Wayne County Community College, located in the heart of metropolitan Detroit, reflected the impact and importance of unions in Michigan. The impact of labor unions in Michigan had a significant educational, economic, social and political influence on the establishment of Wayne County Community College.

The United Automobile Workers (UAW) union had a bargaining unit at the College, which evolved out of a group called the Worker's Liberation Association. Records indicate that the first labor contract negotiated between the College and UAW Local 1796 occurred in 1972. This initial agreement covered the time frame from July 1, 1969 through June 39, 1974. The UAW represented all clerical and support staff of the College with the exception of those individuals who were privy to confidential information dealing with the collective bargaining process, and/ or College policy or its development.

The Professional and Administrative Association (P&AA) grew out of the need for representation for middle management at the College. The first contract between the College and the Professional and Administrative Association (P&AA) was negotiated in 1972. It covered the period of July 1, 1972 through June 30, 1974. This bargaining unit represented all administrative personnel of the College with the exception of those classified at the level of dean or higher, as well as those classifications deemed executive.

The first contract between Wayne County Community College and the American Federation of Teachers (AFT Local 2000) covered the period from September 1, 1972 through August 31, 1974. This bargaining unit represented all full-time and part-time instructors of the College.

CHAPTER VIII
THE FIRST GRADUATING CLASS

The Commencement of the first class of graduates from Wayne County Community College was on Saturday, June 6, 1970, at the Detroit Institute of Arts. The Honorable Governor G. Mennen Williams, General Chairman of the Area Citizens Advisory Council, delivered the Commencement address.

The graduating class was composed of nine proud individuals: Clyde W. Churchill, Wyandotte, Michigan and Marjorie Glander, Detroit, Michigan—Valedictorians; Allen A. Cholger, Detroit, Michigan; Marianne J. Curran, Dearborn Heights, Michigan; Ivory Adreena Gilmore, Detroit, Michigan; Betty Jane Kadar, Millington, Tennessee; Edward Lawrence Kammer, Allen Park, Michigan; Willie David McClung, Detroit, Michigan; and Eugene L. Moses, Westland, Michigan.

Clyde Churchill attended Eastern Michigan University and completed courses at an extension center of the University of Michigan prior to attending Wayne County Community College. While attending, he decided that Business Administration would be his major and planned to complete his education at Eastern Michigan University.

Marjorie Glander attended Macomb County Community College, Wayne State University, and completed some correspondence courses from the University of Michigan prior to attending Wayne County Community College. She considered both music and nursing since she planned on continuing her studies at Wayne State University. She found the College to be both accessible and reasonable.

Allan A. Cholger attended Central Michigan University prior to enrolling and graduating from Wayne County Community College.

Marianne J. Curran attended Michigan State University before enrolling at Wayne County Community College in Detroit. She planned to continue her education at Eastern Michigan University and major in Home Economics. She found the College to be both convenient and academically sound.

Betty Jane Kadar attended many schools across the country— Orange Coast College, California; Long Beach City College, California; University of Michigan, Oakland County Community College, and Henry Ford Community College, Michigan. At Wayne County Community College, she was able to draw her many educational experiences together and earn a degree.

Ivory Adreena Gilmore attended Highland Park Community College in Highland Park, Michigan where she was part of a Higher Education Opportunity Committee Program prior to attending Wayne County Community College. She planned to continue her education at Michigan State University, majoring in elementary education. She found the College's satellite location very convenient and the tuition very reasonable.

While attending Eastern Michigan University, Edward Lawrence Kammer needed to be hospitalized because of a physical condition. His doctor would not allow him to return to Eastern that semester. His sister registered him for three classes at the College at a center very near his home. His sister attended the classes for him until he was able to attend. He returned to Eastern Michigan University in 1970, but continued to take Business Law at the College so that he could also earn an Associate's degree as well.

Willie David McClung attended Miles College in Birmingham, Alabama prior to enrolling at Wayne County Community College. To take the necessary classes for graduation, he attended two centers in 1970. He planned to attend Wayne State University and major in Business Administration. He believed the courses in Business Administration would help him as a pastor.

Eugene L. Moses began his career as a teacher. Next, he worked at a bank and then attended law school at night. When the Great Depression occurred, the bank closed and he was no longer able to attend night school. After a number of temporary jobs, he got a job at Wayne County General Hospital. After working at the hospital for 30 years, he retired. It was at this point in his life, 67 years old, that he enrolled at Wayne County Community College. He planned to take additional classes at the College or continue his education by enrolling at Eastern Michigan University.

CHAPTER IX
FINANCING WAYNE COUNTY
COMMUNITY COLLEGE:

Selling Bonds, Owning Property
and Master Facilities Plan

In recognition of the College's struggle and success, in 1971 the Michigan legislature and Governor G. Mennen Williams mandated a one-quarter mill allocation from the County Board of Commissioners. This allocation temporarily alleviated some of the College's more pressing financial needs. In 1973, the state provided additional assistance by enacting legislation designed to place the College on equal funding basis with other public community colleges. In addition, the legislature granted the community colleges the authority to purchase property. House Bills 4793 and 4787 had a decided effect on the future shape of Wayne County Community College.

In 1974, the successful sale of bonds for capital outlay provided initial funding for the construction of five major instructional centers. The second successful bond sale in 1976 accelerated facility developments. This successful endeavor served as a catalyst for the development of an administrative structure that conformed with the physical plant configurations. The objective of the planners was to consummate the plan prior to the opening of the Downriver Campus in August of 1979 as outlined in the Five Year Master Facilities Plan of Wayne County Community College (1973-1978).

The Five Year Master Facilities Plan was a major step in the College's growth. It came about as a result of the Michigan legislature authorizing Wayne County to levy up to 1.000 mills for debt retirement. This permitted the creation of five regions, each headquartered in one of the major instructional centers. The Plan, initiated in 1973 and completed by 1978, included the size and type of facility, the location, and the projected costs of construction, equipment, furnishings and site acquisition. This complete layout is documented in the Wayne County Community College Five Year Master Facilities Plan of 1973.

CHAPTER X
ADMINISTRATIVE DECENTRALIZATION/
REORGANIZATION

Chris Argyris and Donald A. Schoen in <u>Organizational Learning:</u> <u>A Theory of Action Perspective,</u> (1978), defined reorganization this way, *"...organizational learning, in a deeper sense, may refer to the processes by which organizational category-schemes, models, images, or cognitive modes are transformed in response to error, anomaly, or inconsistency."* Dr. Willie J. Kimmons in <u>Black Administrators in Public Community</u> <u>Colleges (Self-Perceived Role and Status 1977),</u> explains that *"From the average layman's point of view, reorganization is a restructuring of an organization (or model or plan) based on errors or mistakes noted in the organization, model or plan."* In this chapter, Wayne County Community College took the necessary steps to reorganize its administrative structure to increase its effectiveness, efficiency and to make the College current and competitive in its instructional delivery system.

Waye County Community College identified regional decentralization and administrative reorganization as key strategies to ensure continued efforts to improve the quality of its educational programs. In 1976, therefore, the College designed plans that would develop and reallocate services and resources to meet the needs of new campus/satellite center configurations.

With the consent of the Board of Trustees, on January 31, 1977, a regional campus pilot governance model was implemented at the Greenfield Campus. The administrative team of this pilot project had representatives from academic, administration, finance and student services divisions. The administrative team implemented policies at the Greenfield Campus and its satellite centers. The project had a dual reporting system. Each administrator reported to his or her appropriate divisional vice-president, as well as to the Regional Core Director/Dean.

Later in that same year, a comprehensive decentralized plan for every division was adopted. Wayne County Community College became the fastest growing community college in Michigan. Its beginnings and continued growth have been dynamic and unlike any community college in the state. Its determination to survive is unequaled in the country. Quality open-door higher education provided in accessible locations at the lowest possible cost is the College's hallmark. This goal fueled enrollment increases that ultimately mandated the construction of five regional core instructional centers.

Given the reality of a fast moving and major capital outlay program operative at Wayne County Community College, the necessity to consider new organizational models for effective management became more apparent each day. In July of 1976, the Executive Committee of the College addressed a memorandum to the Board of Trustees which spoke to the need for a new and more appropriate management model tailored to the unique features of the College. One of the ways information could be gathered to aid in decision-making was through the launching of a prototype pilot program at the Greenfield Campus within the Northwest Region. The Board of Trustees at its January 31, 1977 meeting adopted the prototype concept and the assumptions upon which it is based.

The first Pilot Team was put in place on January 31, 1977, and ended on May 31, 1977. A second team was installed on June 1, 1977. Since June1, 1977, there have been numerous meetings, studies, reports, research efforts and a representative task force functioning to provide as much input as possible. Also, Wayne County Community College acquired the consultant services of Professor Joseph Consand of the University of Michigan. He interacted with the Executive Committee, the Pilot Team, The Reorganization Administrative Decentralization Task Force and other involved personnel.

The experiences of the reorganized structure of 1977, along with investigations into the literature and other institutions' experiences have led to the administration to several major conclusions. The first is that instructional effectiveness should be the primary goal of the decentralized structure. "Contrary to many beliefs regarding the process of education, the very heart of the educational program is not the budget, but the school curriculum..."[2] the second is reorganization is not a single-phase process. Like a hypothesis, it must be tested, validated, revised and retested. Only after thorough evaluation and modification is the process complete. Wayne County Community College remains in a state of transition. Reorganization promises the reward of an efficient, stable, smoothly functional organization.

Administrative structure of the College

Administrative leadership of Wayne County Community College had been quite fluid. The College has been able, nevertheless, to maintain its credibility and to provide leadership and educational opportunities for the citizens of Wayne County. This has been demonstrated by the successful visits during the North Central Accreditation Association reviews from 1970-1983. The reviews indicated that the College had great potential and made tremendous strides in improving the quality of instruction in its educational program. The North Central Accreditation Association further stated that Wayne County Community College is a dynamic institution that has been changing and growing throughout its life in spite of turmoil and political struggles. This is not to say that change implies dynamism, only that a college cannot remain the same within a changing environment. As the leadership changed, the College, as a whole, has changed in a positive direction. As Kimmons stated in his book, <u>Black Administrators in Public Community Colleges,</u> (1977), "Energy must be expended at all levels of the organization to relate its internal processes with the needs of its constituency and offers several approaches to measuring an organization's effectiveness. One factor is its ability to satisfy its constituents or those individuals or groups that have a vested interest in the organization. "From the structural perspective, organizational learning has to do with change of structure (Kimmons, 1977). In order to ensure that instruction is the primary goal of a newly installed regional structure, change in the College system is essential." I think Wayne County Community College is taking the necessary steps to restore its future.

In 1976, under Aid to Developing Institutions, the College received a two million dollar Department of Health, Education and Welfare (H.E.W.) grant to implement improvements in academic affairs, student services and management. In the academic service area, the College expanded the learning resources center and cooperative education, developed a special needs curriculum' and in conjunction with Wayne State University, constructed a transportable academic student follow-up model.

In the student services area, The College expanded student services in career counseling, academic and personal counseling, assessment counseling and support, financial aid delivery and student records. In the area of management, the College emphasized improvements in planning, management, evaluation and management information systems, and jointly, with the University of Michigan, staffing and staff development.

CHAPTER XI
NORTH CENTRAL ACCREDITATION ASSOCIATION

Visits during the Early Years of the College

Wayne County Community College was accredited by the North Central Accreditation Association. The following is a chronology of information related to the College's accreditation history:

1970 (April): Granted Correspondent status

1973 (July): College became candidate for accreditation under new policy

1973 (September): College submitted biennial visit report in preparation for evaluation

1976 (March): After an extensive site visit, the North Central Accreditation Association granted Wayne County Community College membership in the Association through the Commission on Institutions of Higher Education as an associate degree granting institution, and scheduled an evaluation visit within three years. This recognition was the culmination of a five year goal. It was an official public confirmation that Wayne County Community College was an institution of educational quality and depth. This affirmation was conferred after an extensive self-study and accreditation team evaluation.

1978 (November): The College submitted a 1977-78 Institutional Self-Study Report for reaffirmation of accreditation with the North Central Association of Colleges and Schools. This self-study report was to provide evidence, an assessment of the College's mission attainment, to demonstrate that Wayne County Community College had increased in strength educationally over the past years and that the institution was sufficiently strong, based on its educational programs, to have its status of accreditation reaffirmed and continued over a longer period of time.

1983 March: The College was scheduled for another site visitation by the North Central Accreditation Association of Colleges and Schools.

CHAPTER XII
LAUNCHING OF FIVE MAJOR REGIONAL CORE CENTERS/CAMPUSES

Inherent in the College's mission was to provide a meaningful quality education for all of its students. The decentralization of facilities was an essential element in the College carrying out its mission. The plan for five regional locations was designed to achieve the following:

1) Provide for a more equitable distribution of programs and services throughout the entire service district.
2) Allow for a more efficient system in the administration and supervision of programs and services throughout the entire service district.
3) Gain broad citizen support throughout the entire service district by providing a visible facility within each of the five proposed regions with which the community could identify.
4) Provide required facilities to expand specialized vocational-technical and health career instructional programs throughout the entire service district.
5) Work cooperatively with the various K-12 school districts, other colleges and universities, as well as other related agencies in the effective utilization of facilities.

The five regional core centers include: the Downriver Center, the Downtown Center, the Northwestern Center (Greenfield Center), the Western Center, and the Eastern Center.

CHAPTER XIII
INSTITUTIONAL CRISES AND CONCERNS OF WAYNE COUNTY COMMUNITY COLLEGE IN THE 1990'S

From a difficult and abnormal birth, through a battered childhood to the current state of an older adolescent with potential for a confused, troubled and unproductive adulthood, Wayne County Community College has emerged. The direction that the College takes during this critical period (October 1990-December 1991) will determine its destiny. Current crises to be resolved include:

1) College apparently did not have the confidence of the community
2) Negative publicity resulted in the defeat of an important millage in August 1990
3) The College's image was a serious problem and public confidence was low
4) Board's policy of loose control, improprieties with regard to overpayments to faculty and staff members, and mismanagement of appropriated funds
5) The widely held perception that the Office of the President at Wayne County Community College was ineffective and unstable
6) The negative publicity surrounding Wayne County Community College continued to undermine the future growth and development of the College. This is nowhere more clearly evident than in a statement by Wayne County Community College President, Rafael Cortada who, in noting that problems at the College have received a high degree of media coverage, while positive programs, such as the expansion of student and health services, the initiation of athletic programs run by part0time coaches, and the new shuttle service have not been highlighted. Cortada stated, "We've done so much good and received so little credit: (Zinner, March 1991; Twardon, April 1991). The result

39

is Wayne County Community College remains the only community college in the state that is not supported by its own millage.

7) Failure of Wayne County Community College to define lines of demarcation between policy development by the governing board and administrative operations

8) Projected reductions in funding provide the setting for restructuring of College operations. Board of Trustees approved and early retirement program. About 75 voluntary retirements are projected. This coincides with reduction of about 50-60 positions in the restructuring, and may eliminate the need for involuntary separations. As the Board moves forward with reforms, a renewed effort to secure millage support is projected for fall, 1992. Additionally, 1992 will be the time when the terms of all of the district trustees will expire. (Cortada, April 1991).

9) There was a crisis in constituency support and community Image. As reported earlier, the College never gained a voted millage and had, unfortunately, had periodic series of negative mass media coverage. Such negative press had been around the changes in the Office of the President. The total amount of negative mass media coverage from the firing of a series of presidents over a short period of time was a particularly damaging two-year period and continues as of this writing. The realistic chances of a millage campaign being successful now are nonexistent. An even deeper and troubling problem is the decrease in enrollment. Enrollment for 1990-1991 fell from 25,000 to 11,000 students. There were 15,000 empty seats (Cortada, 1991).

10) The college had to come to grips, successfully, with resolving the struggle between central versus regional administration. The College developed a regional pilot in 1977, implemented a regional plan in 1978, and reverted back to a centralized operation in 1982. Only in the first instance was substantial outside consultative

assistance used. Also, the regional system, which was used for over four years, always had a shared authority and responsibility which is different from other multi-unit urban colleges. Chief campus executives shared authority over their regional-based subordinate supervisors with central executives who normally would be considered "staff" rather than "line" officers in other institutions. Regardless of one's organizational preferences, the College had to bring the conflict to an efficient, stable, responsive and academically respectable resolution.

11) In spite of the fact that the institution's birth and early growth was directly attributable to the political process, the College must now adhere to the very best and time proven Principles of Higher Education generally and the Community College philosophy in particular in order not only to prosper but to survive. The College must join its sister institutions in adopting similar processes, procedures, Board practices and create the learning environment which exists at other colleges. While WC3 was a unique and had a number of special missions, it must also be a regular part of the academic community. Striving toward instructional goals of quality education and developmental support within the normal framework of the guiding principles of higher education was the only answer. Political goals or initiatives must be subjugated to the long-term good of the institution.

12) The College was over-dependent on state and federal funding. Not having a local voted millage (the College has only a .25 mil established by the Legislature), the College was automatically forced to be over-dependent on federal and state funds. The College had to seek out and develop creative alliances which would help to stabilize the College financially. Contracted for training expanded continuing education programs and similar efforts could be possible. The rudiments of such alliances already exist and the College had experienced admirable success in a number of these projects.

13) There is no systematic result-oriented professional development effort or plan at the College.
14) The College was literally a prisoner of its outside computing contractor. Under present conditions, no college-hired people were being trained or would ever be trained.

Failure to restore public confidence, failure of voters to pass a millage in 1992, and failure to reform Wayne County Community College operations both administrative and within, Board of Trustees' failure to secure support of the Michigan legislature during the interim and the anticipated passage of the 1992 millage, and to demonstrate Wayne County Community College's accountability to the public served as other serious threats to the College's future.

The 1990 WJBK-TV news editorial report by J. Weaver stated, "Historically, money has been at the root of the Board's actions as manifest by its policy of loose control, improprieties with regard to overpayments to faculty and staff members, and mismanagement of appropriated funds." For example, an article appearing in an issue of The Detroit News documented that state auditors investigated Wayne County Community College pay records and alleged that thousands of dollars were spent in suspected overpayments to Wayne County Community College employees for time spent performing special assignments and extra duties. In one case, "over a two and one-half period, a faculty member, in addition to an annual salary of about $50,000, received $84,500 for special assignments and teaching extra classes", (Twardon, 1990 p. 8A;). Morganfield (1990) further reported that Michigan auditors investigated pay records at Wayne County Community College and searched for suspected overpayments to faculty members who were allowed to perform other college-related jobs. The investigation, which involved thousands of dollars in overpayments, came after a state audit criticized Wayne County Community College's decision to invest millions of dollars in bond money instead of using it for proposed construction projects. Twardon (1990) reported similar concerns about Wayne County Community College

Board mismanagement when he stated that an investigation by the Michigan state auditor general found Wayne County Community College had issued $24 million dollars in bonds for projects it had never built. After securing property taxes to pay for the bonds, the College invested the money and used the income as operating funds.

The negative publicity surrounding Wayne County Community College continued to thwart the College's efforts to secure a millage from the citizens of Wayne County. The result is Wayne County Community College remains the only community college in the state that is not supported by its own millage. In the early years of the College a decision was made by the state legislature to eliminate over a five year period, at the rate of @2 million per year, @10.4 million in state aid, which served in lieu of millage support. This proposal became effective July 1, 1991. Low public confidence was evidenced again when the voters rejected in August of 1990, a millage tax levy, that would have replaced the $10.4 million in state aid that Wayne County Community College may have lost due to state budget cuts (Musial & Ball, 1990).

Other educational institutions in this country would have succumbed to such political, economic union and social pressures.

The fact that Wayne County Community College has prevailed suggests that it not only will survive, but will thrive in the coming years to be a viable institution of higher learning. This is exemplified in the statement by former Wayne County Community College Board of Trustees Chairman, Dr. Charles Morton that the Board would amend any behavior and make the reforms needed to ensure the stability and success of Wayne County Community College (Musial, 1990). In addition, as of March 1991, Wayne County Community College Board of Trustees moved to strengthen internal controls and to streamline operations according to recommendations by state auditors, as well as, those resulting from the Board's own management analysis (Ball, 1991).

In addition, according to J. Weaver, August, 1990, in a WJBK-TV news editorial, he stated that Wayne County Community College's problems may be due in part by the College's Board of Trustees, such as decision making that led to negative publicity that resulted in the defeat of an important millage vote. The college's image was a serious problem and public confidence was low.

CHAPTER XIV
STRENGTHS OF WAYNE COUNTY
COMMUNITY COLLEGE

a) Excellent teaching and Scholarship among faculty
b) Important contributions the college made to the county residents
c) Added economic development in the region
d) During Temple's Administration (1985-1990)
   a) Hired competent senior administrative staff
   b) Rebuilt public confidence in the college as documented by a survey commissioned by Michigan State Department of Education
   c) Restored full accreditation by the North Centra
   d) Reversed the steep decline in enrollment
   e) Forged a close partnership with business and industry
   (DR. TEMPLES'S LETTER OF 4/29/91)
1) During Cortada's Administration (1990-1995)
   a) Secured legislative approval for continuation of $10.4 million tax grant for the college
   b) Completed analysis showing that decentralization caused inflation of salaries and non-teaching staff resulting in Board of Trustees linking staff to student ratios eliminating 50 management positions
   c) Board initiated financial and management initiatives
   d) Board approved centralized reporting
   e) Board approves specialization for vocational technical programs on each of the campuses
   f) Board approves early retirement plan which most staff accepts
   (Dr. CONTRADA'S LETTER OF 10/1/1990)

CHAPTER XV
WEAKNESSES OF WAYNE COUNTY
COMMUNITY COLLEGE

1. College is over-dependent on state and federal funding
2. College personnel possess a low level of computer literacy and current software is outdated and there are no plans to purchase new software at this time.
3. During Temple's Administration (1985-1990)
   a. Dominance of unionism as a political force
   b. Political antics of Board Members
   c. Board members failure to grasp the role of Boardman ship
   d. Political interference of the city of Detroit
   e. Failure of the college to build public confidence
   f. Having a rapid turnover of College presidents
   g. Lack of qualifications of College Presidents
   (DR. TEMPLES' LETTER OF 4/29/91)

CHAPTER XVI
STRATEGIC PLAN FOR WAYNE COUNTY COMMUNITY COLLEGE (CORTADA, 1990)

1. Cuts in administrative staff – New hires at Wayne County Community College's five campuses would be permitted only if enrollment rises.
2. A revamped system for registering and tracking students, who would have minimum academic progress to stay enrolled (A student who enrolls in 12 or more credit hours in any given semester must complete at least 50% of the credit hours attempted with a grade of "C" or better).
3. Possible consolidation of programs offered at more than one campus. For example, consolidation of nursing laboratories from three Wayne County Community College campuses. According to President Cortada in 1991, if the nursing laboratories were merged, they could save money and gain accreditation. No single nursing program had enough money for an accredited program (Tobin, April 1991).
4. Scrapping an archaic computer system that some say is partially to blame for administrative chaos. The system relies on software programs written in 1968 and 1972. President Cortada predicts that if the above strategic plan does not materialize, Wayne County voters will reject any new millage request and "the College's demise will come soon after" (Tobin, April 1991).

CHAPTER XVII
SUMMARY OF THE WAYNE COUNTY COMMUNITY COLLEGE DISTRICT 1995-2016

Wayne County Community College has grown from its humble beginnings in 1964 to the current state of great growth and development in 2016 under the leadership of a visionary, trained and competent leader, Dr. Curtis Ivery. Dr. Ivery assumed the Presidency in 1995 and some twenty-one years later, has completely changed the entire organizational structure of what was known as Wayne County Community College to Wayne County Community College District.

The organizational structure reflected the change from a centralized structure to a decentralized structure with the five educational campuses headed by a Chief Executive Officer with the title of Campus President and the central office chief executive officer with the title of Chancellor. This structure changed by Dr. Ivery brought Wayne County Community College into the current organizational structure that was compatible with today's trends with most two year colleges in the country. The Chancellor serves as the "District Administrator" for the entire organization that comprises what is now known as the Wayne County Community College District. This organizational structure is composed of the following:

1. District Administrative Office
2. Downriver Educational Campus
3. Downtown Educational Campus
4. Eastern Educational Campus
5. Northwestern Educational Campus
6. Western Educational Campus
7. Lutheran His East Extension Site

These educational campuses are strategically located in every section of the County of Wayne. Wayne County the third largest county in the United States serving the largest Arab population outside of the Middle East. With the five major educational campuses, the Wayne County Community College District reflects the ethnic and cultural make up of its constituents, making it one of the most diversified community college district in the United States.

Under the leadership of Dr. Curtis Ivery, District Chancellor, Wayne County Community College District today has become a world-class educational institution of higher learning that people of all races can be proud of. The general public, college administrative staff, faculty, students, Board of Trustees and concerned supporters are all to be commended for their long and tireless efforts to bring the college into the twenty first century in the area of educational stability and reform.

The story of the Wayne County Community College District is interwoven into the moral fabric of the City of Detroit, Michigan. Because I believe that Detroit right now is a great American story. No city has had more influence in the country's economic and social evolution. Detroit was the birthplace of both the industrial age and the nation's middle class along with the city's rise and fall----and struggle to rise again are a window into the challenges facing all of modern America including:

1. urban planning;
2. corruption with unions;
3. political problems in city hall;
4. the crisis of manufacturing;
5. the rise and fall of the automobile industry;
6. lingering role of race and class in our society;
7. the struggle for affordable health care and education;

All of these challenges have happened in the most extreme cases in Detroit, Michigan. Racial tension, poor educational systems, crime, disgraced politicians and woeful auto industry brought Detroit, Michigan to its' knees.

Racial tensions exploded into rioting in July 1967, killing 43 people and sending thousands of white Detroiters to the suburbs. The

49

exodus institutionalize racial divisions that have only hardened since. Suburbanization turned Detroit into a majority African-American city, and elected its' first black mayor, The Honorable Coleman Young (1973-1993). But, in 1964, three years prior to city riots, A Citizen Advisory Committee made up of concerned citizens, was formed by Wayne County Intermediate School District. They conducted a feasibility study to assess whether a community college was needed. This was the true beginning of the birth of The Wayne County Community College District in Detroit, Michigan.

As a testimony of the history of the Wayne County Community College District's beginning, this is the first attempt to document the strengths and weaknesses of human beings in turning around an educational institution under adverse and unusual circumstances. Wayne County Community College District like the city of Detroit has been misunderstood, underrepresented, under-funded, underreported, stereotyped, divided and exploited for decades.

The story of Wayne County Community College District is one of continued innovation, growth and development in serving the Detroit Metropolitan area and citizenry. It was created in 1964 by a Citizen Advisory Committee to provide educational service.

Under the leadership of the former mayor of Detroit, The Honorable Dave Bing (2009) and the visionary leadership of Chancellor Curtis L. Ivery, I saw tremendous growth and significant changes in the future of Wayne County Community College District and the city of Detroit. These two outstanding Americans during their tenure brought a sense of instant credibility and stability to both the college and the city. The title of this book, <u>The Making of an Urban Community College in a Union and Political Environment: A Historical Perspective of Wayne County Community College District, Detroit, Michigan (1964-2016)</u> is true to form. This historical overview has been a

50

work of love, commitment and dedication to all those who paid the ultimate sacrifice to continue this city and college's legacy.

Thank you and God Bless in the struggle,
Dr. Willie J Greer Kimmons
Former Campus President Downtown Campus
Wayne County Community College District (1979-1983)

BIBLIOGRAPHY

Argyris, C. & Schoen, D.A. (1978). Organizational learning: A theory of Action Perspective. Addison Wesley, 325.

Ball, Z. (1991, March 28). WAYNE COUNTY COMMUNITY COLLEGE OKs tighter controls: Trustees take action on audit findings. Detroit Free Press.

Cortada, R. (1991, April 9). Challenges and opportunities facing Wayne County Community College, October 1, 1990 to April 1, 1990. Unpublished letter from Rafael Cortada, President Wayne County Community College, Detroit.

Keene, R. (1964). Comprehensive plans for the organization of community college districts in Wayne County, Michigan. Unpublished doctoral dissertation, Wayne State University, Detroit.

Kimmons, W. (1977). Black Administrators in Public Community Colleges: Self-Perceived Role and Status. A Heartstone Book, Carlton Press, Inc. New York, New York.

Morganfield, R. (1990, August 29). State investigates WAYNE COUNTY COMMUNITY COLLEGE pay records: Overpayments to faculty members alleged. The Detroit News. pp. 1A, 2A.

Musial, R. & Ball, Z. (1990, August 29). WAYNE COUNTY COMMUNITY COLLEGE panel fires official who called in state auditors. Detroit Free Press.

Musial, R. (1990, August 29). Community college audit finds problems. Detroit Free Press.

Michigan State Board of Education Minutes, 1964-1980.

Report of an Examination Visit for Correspondent Status for Wayne County Community College for North Central Association of Colleges and Schools, 1970.

Okrent, Daniel (2009). "The Tragedy of Detroit, How a Great City Fell and How It Can Rise Again", Time Magazine Special Report

Sims Howard and Associates, Architects and Planners. Wayne County Community College Facilities Plan 1978.

Strobel, E. (1975). Wayne County Community College, A History, Establishment, and Early Development in the Metropolitan Detroit Selling. (Doctoral Dissertation), Wayne State University.

Tanner, K.C. (1973). Design for Educational Planning. Heath Lexington, 9. Wayne County Community College Citizens Advisory Council, 1969-1982.

Tobin, J. (1991, March 17). Salary padding charged at WAYNE COUNTY COMMUNITY COLLEGE. The Detroit News. pp. 1C.

Tobin, J. (1991, April 1). Overhaul troubled WAYNE COUNTY COMMUNITY COLLEGE or it will die, president tells board. The Detroit News. 1C

Twardon, L. (1990, August 29). WAYNE COUNTY COMMUNITY COLLEGE trustees fire 'whistleblower'. The Detroit News. pp. 1A, 8A.

Twardon, L. (1991, April 11). Troubled WC3 cuts 50 nonteaching positions. The Detroit News.

Wayne County Community College, Annual Report, 1976.

Wayne County Community College, Annual Report, 1979/80.

Wayne County Community College, <u>First Decade Report</u>, 1967-1977.

Wayne County Community College, <u>Institutional Self-Study Report</u>, 1977-78.

Weaver, J. (1990, September 6, 6:30 P.M.). WJBK-TV Eyewitness News editorial: Wayne County Community College. <u>Radio TV Reports</u>.

Zinner, J. D. (1991, March 31). College braving financial storm. <u>Enterprise</u>.

APPENDICES

APPENDIX A

Dr. Tom Waters Former Interim President Permission letter to conduct the Research Study of the History of Wayne County Community College September 28, 1982

Wayne
County
Community
College

801 W. Fort Street
Detroit, Michigan
48226

Telephone: (313) 496-2510

Thomas F. Waters, Ph
Interim President

September 28, 1982

Dr. Willie J. Kimmons
1431 Washington Boulevard
Trolley Plaza — Apt 1115
Detroit, MI 48226

Dear Dr. Kimmons:

I am pleased to inform you that the Board of Trustees, at
its September 15, 1982 meeting, approved your request for
educational leave.

One of the conditions of that leave was that you would work
in collaboration with Dr. Julius Brown on developing a book
on Wayne County Community College. This would view Wayne
County Community College from a historical perspective and
emphasize and catalog its positive accomplishments.

As we discussed, your plan of approach is basically the
following:

    a)   September 15, 1982 - December 15, 1982:

         Data gathering and interviews.

    b)   January 1, 1983 - February 28, 1983:

         Preliminary tabulation and assessment.

    c)   March 1, 1983 - May 31, 1983:

         Writing, editing, and revising.

    d)   June 1, 1983 - July 15, 1983:

         Final production.

Dr. Willie J. Kimmons
September 28, 1982
Page 2

I am agreeing on behalf of the College to the following set
of circumstances:

1. Open and complete access to faculty, staff and
    public records of the institution during your data
    gathering process.

2. Moderate use of faculty office facilities during
    the course of your study.

3. Moderate use of assistance will be provided when
    available; workstudy, etc., to assist in the
    transcriptions and reproduction. It is understood
    that this will be at no cost to the College.

To accomplish these goals, I will make this letter available
to regional personnel and forward the attached letter from
you to College employees requesting input.

As I have said to you on numerous occasions, it has been a
pleasure working with you in our various roles at the
College and I wish you the best of luck in this endeavor and
the future.

Sincerely,

Thomas F. Waters
Interim President

attachment a/s

Wayne
County
Community
College

801 W. Fort Street
Detroit, Michigan
48226
(313) 496 2500

September 28, 1982

Dear College Employee:

As you are probably aware, we are on professional leave for the next ten months. One of the obligations of that leave is to develop a book on Wayne County Community College emphasizing the history of the College and catalog its positive accomplishments.

We have secured permission from the administration to conduct our interviews at the College and contact resource persons within the remainder of the Fall Semester (September 15, 1982 to December 15, 1982). We are asking your assistance in the identification of successfully completed projects or initiatives. Please send such information to Ms. Frances Peace at the Downtown Campus.

Over the years we know that Wayne County Community College has made definite contributions to higher education by providing opportunities and training to former and present students. Your help will be greatly appreciated.

Sincerely,

Julius R. Brown, Ph.D.

Willie J. Kimmons, Ph.D.

APPENDIX B

PERSONAL INTERVIEWS AND CONTRIBUTORS

Ms. Ruby Butts

Former Alumni Activist; Distinguished Graduate; Staff Wayne State University, College of Education

Dr. Arthur Carter

Former President, Northwest Campus, Wayne County Community College Currently, Superintendent of Highland Park Schools, Highland Park, Michigan

Former Senator Arthur Cartwright

Former Michigan State Senator, from Detroit Michigan; Sponsor and Supporter for Senate Bill 630, August 1, 1967, which was the creation of Wayne County Community College

Mr. Claude Chapman

Former President, American Federation of Teachers (AFT – Local 2000), Counselor and Professor

Dr. William Colovas

Former Vice President for Instruction and Former Vice President for Administration Wayne County Community College

MS. Swanie Colvin

Former Secretary, Wayne County Community College

Dr. Rafael Cortada	Former President, Wayne County Community College
Ms. Amanda Davis	Former Director of Student Services, Wayne County Community College
Mr. Walter Douglas	Former President, New Detroit, Inc.
Ms. Juanita Ford	Longest Serving Member of Wayne County Community College Board of Trustees 1975-2010
Dr. Stella Fulgham	Former Professor and Assistant Dean of Instruction, Wayne County Community College, Downtown Campus
Dr. Della Goodwin	Former Dean of Nursing, Wayne County Community College
Mr. William Herbert	Former Interim President, Wayne County Community College District and Executive, Blue Cross-Blue Shield
Dr. Jacqueline Hodges	Former President, Downtown Campus, Wayne County Community College
Former State Senator David Holmes	Former Supporter, Wayne County Community College in the State Senate; Former Vice Chairperson of the State Appropriation Committee, State of Michigan

Ms. Margaret Horn

Former Secretary to the Board
of Trustees, Member of First
Graduation Committee, Wayne
County Community College

Mr. Thomas Howard, Jr.

Former Chief Operational Officer
for Finance and Administration
and Former Director of
Purchasing, Wayne County
Community College District

Mr. Murray Jackson

First Chief Executive Officer
of Wayne County Community
College District, and Professor,
University of Michigan

Dr. Arthur Jefferson

Former Superintendent, Detroit
Public Schools and Staff
Person Representing Detroit
Public Schools on New Detroit
Education Committee

Dr. Conrad Mallett

Former Vice President for
Academic Affairs, Wayne County
Community College

Dr. Daniel Manthe

Former Associate
Superintendent, Wayne County
Intermediate School District;
Lobbyist, Wayne County
Intermediate School District

Ms. Betty Morgan

Former Secretary Wayne County
Community College

Rev. Charles Morton

Former Minister, Metropolitan
Baptist Church, Detroit, Michigan
and Former Member, State
Board of Education

Mr. Alfred Pelham	Former Interim President, Wayne County Community College District, Former Director of Budget and Finance, Wayne County; Developer of First Budgetary Process, Wayne State University; First Controller, City of Detroit; Former Chairman of the Board, Great Lakes Mutual Insurance Company
Dr. John Porter	Former President, Eastern Michigan University; Former State Superintendent of Public Instruction and Former Superintendent, Detroit Public Schools
Mr. Sammie Rice	Chief Operational Officer for Facilities and Former President of United Automobile Workers (UAW)Local 1796, Wayne County Community College District
The Honorable George Romney	Former Governor, State of Michigan
Dr. Glenwood Ross	Former Professor, Wayne County Community College, Downtown Campus
Mr. Arthur Rowland	Former Professor, Wayne County Community College Northwest Campus
Dr. Frank Samuels	Former Provost, Vice President for Academic Affairs, Wayne County Community College

Mr. Richard Simmons	Former President, Wayne County Community College District, Former Deputy Mayor, City of Detroit; Chief Deputy Director, Michigan Mental Health Department
Mr. James Sleet	Former Administrator and Business Manager, Wayne County Community College
Mr. Robert Spencer	Former President, Detroit Economic Growth Corporation and Former Executive Vice President, New Detroit, Inc.
Mr. Richard Stoll	Former Registrar, Professor and Member First Graduation Committee Wayne County Community College
Ms. Kathleen Strauss	Former Staff, Michigan Association of School Boards; First Chairperson, Board of Trustees, Wayne County Community College
Dr. Eugene Stobel	Professor, and Chairman First Graduation Committee, Wayne County Community College
Dr. Mildred Tanner	Former Dean, Student Services, and Professor, Wayne County Community College, Downtown Campus
Dr. Ronald Temple	Former President, Wayne County Community College District

Dr. Richard M. Turner	Former Interim President, Wayne County Community College
Ms. Harriet Thomas	Former Secretary to Presidents and Staff, Personnel Department, Wayne County Community College
Mr. Lynn Townsend	Former Chairman of Board, Chrysler Corporation and First Chairman, Education Committee, New Detroit, Inc.
Ms. Sharon Tye	Former Secretary and Member First Graduation Committee, Wayne County Community College
Dr. Thelma Vriend	Former Vice President, Student Services, Wayne County Community College
Ms. Jane Wagner	Former Secretary and Administrator, Wayne County Community College, Eastern Campus
Ms. Beverly Walton	Former Secretary, Wayne County Community College
Dr. Thomas Waters	Former Interim President and Professor, Wayne County Community College

Former State
Representative
Juanita Watkins

Former Michigan State Representative and Former Wayne County Community College Supporter in the House of Representative, from Detroit, Michigan

The Honorable G Mennen Williams

Former Governor, State of Michigan

Dr. Reginald Wilson

Former President, Wayne County Community College

The Honorable Coleman Young

Former Mayor, City of Detroit, Michigan

APPENDIX C

CHIEF EXECUTIVE OFFICERS OF WAYNE COUNTY COMMUNITY COLLEGE 1968-2016

Mr. Murray E. Jackson:
Executive Secretary/Director - August 1968 to November 1969;
Acting President - November 1969 to October 1970;
President - October 1970 to June 1971.

Mr. Alfred M. Pelham:
Interim President - March 1971 to September 1971.

Dr. Reginald Wilson:
President - October 1971 to May 1980.

Mr. William G. Herbert:
Interim President - June 1980 to December 1980.

Mr. Richard Simmons, Jr.:
President - January 1981 to June 1982.

Dr. Thomas F. Waters:
Interim President - June 1982 to February 1983.

Mr. George Bell:
President - March 1983 to December 1983

Dr. Thomas F. Waters:
President - January 1984 to August 1985.

Dr. Ronald Temple:
President - September 1985 to July 1990.

Dr. Richard M. Turner:
Interim President – July 1990 to September 1990

Dr. Rafael Cortada
President - October 1990 to June 1994

Dr. Richard M. Turner:
Interim President – July 1994 to October 1995

**Dr. Curtis L. Ivery: First Chancellor of the New Wayne
County Community College District**
October 1995 to Present

APPENDIX D

MEMBERS OF THE FIRST BOARD OF TRUSTEES, WAYNE COUNTY COMMUNITY COLLEGE May 9, 1966

APPENDIX E

Letters:

1) Dr. Thomas F. Waters, Interim President Wayne County Community College, September 28, 1982
2) Dr. Julius R. Brown and Dr. Willie J. Kimmons, September 28, 1982
3) Dr. George R. Boggs, Former President and CEO, American Association of Community Colleges, June 8, 2009
4) Dr. Rafael L. Cortada, Former President, Wayne County Community College, June 18, 1991
5) Dr. Ronald J. Temple, Former President, Wayne County Community College, January 6, 1992
6) Mrs. Martha Grier, Former Assistant to the Chancellor For Board and Public Relations, April 12, 2007
7) Dr. Richard M. Turner, President Emeritus, Baltimore City Community College, June 2, 2009

September 28, 1982

Dr. Willie J. Kimmons
1831 Washington Boulevard
Trolley Plaza — Apt 1115
Detroit, MI 48226

Dear Dr. Kimmons:

I am pleased to inform you that the Board of Trustees, at
its September 15, 1982 meeting, approved your request for
educational leave.

One of the conditions of that leave was that you would work
in collaboration with Dr. Julius Brown on developing a book
on Wayne County Community College. This would view Wayne
County Community College from a historical perspective and
emphasize and catalog its positive accomplishments.

As we discussed, your plan of approach is basically the
following:

  a)   September 15, 1982 – December 15, 1982:

       Data gathering and interviews.

  b)   January 1, 1983 – February 28, 1983:

       Preliminary tabulation and assessment.

  c)   March 1, 1983 – May 31, 1983:

       Writing, editing, and revising.

  d)   June 1, 1983 – July 15, 1983:

       Final production.

Dr. Willie J. Kimmons
September 28, 1982
Page 2

I am agreeing on behalf of the College to the following set
of circumstances:

1. Open and complete access to faculty, staff and
    public records of the institution during your data
    gathering process.

2. Moderate use of faculty office facilities during
    the course of your study.

3. Moderate use of assistance will be provided when
    available; workstudy, etc., to assist in the
    transcriptions and reproduction. It is understood
    that this will be at no cost to the College.

To accomplish these goals, I will make this letter available
to regional personnel and forward the attached letter from
you to College employees requesting input.

As I have said to you on numerous occasions, it has been a
pleasure working with you in our various roles at the
College and I wish you the best of luck in this endeavor and
the future.

                        Sincerely,

                        Thomas F. Waters
                        Interim President

attachment a/s

Willie Kimmons

Wayne
County
Community
College

801 W. Fort Street
Detroit, Michigan
48226
(313) 496-2500

September 28, 1982

Dear College Employee:

As you are probably aware, we are on professional leave for the next ten months. One of the obligations of that leave is to develop a book on Wayne County Community College emphasizing the history of the College and catalog its positive accomplishments.

We have secured permission from the administration to conduct our interviews at the College and contact resource persons within the remainder of the Fall Semester (September 15, 1982 to December 15, 1982). We are asking your assistance in the identification of successfully completed projects or initiatives. Please send such information to Ms. Frances Peace at the Downtown Campus.

Over the years we know that Wayne County Community College has made definite contributions to higher education by providing opportunities and training to former and present students. Your help will be greatly appreciated.

Sincerely,

Julius R. Brown, Ph.D.

Willie J. Kimmons, Ph.D.

Downriver Region	Western Region	Downtown Region	Eastern Region	Northwest Region
21000 Northline Rd.	9555 Haggerty	1001 W. Fort Street	18300 E. Warren	8551 Greenfield
Taylor 48180	Belleville 48111	Detroit 48226	Detroit 48224	Detroit 48228
Phone: 374-2700	Phone: 699-0200	Phone: 496-2758	Phone: 882-3900	Phone: 943-4000

Subj: **Foreword**
Date: 6/5/2009 6:23:46 P.M. Eastern Daylight Time
From: gboggs@aacc.nche.edu
To: wjkimmons@aol.com
CC: pwilson@aacc.nche.edu

Hello, Willie. It was good to hear from you and to know that you are still contributing in many positive ways. I have attached a draft of the foreword that you requested. I hope that it is what you wanted. Please feel free to edit it as you see fit.

Best wishes.

George

George R. Boggs
President and CEO
American Association of Community Colleges
One Dupont Circle, NW. Suite 410
Washington, DC 20036

202.728.0200, ext. 235
gboggs@aacc.nche.edu
AACC: The Voice of America's Community Colleges
www.aacc.nche.edu

Wayne
County
Community
College

801 W. Fort Street
Detroit, Michigan
48226

Telephone: (313) 496-2510
Fax: (313) 961-9439

Rafael L. Cortada, Ph.D.
President

June 18, 1991

Dr. Willie J. Kimmons
Dean
Gaston College
201 Highway 321 South
Dallas, North Carolina 28034-1499

Dear Dr. Kimmons:

Please accept my apologies for not getting this back
to you earlier. Enclosed is a capsule synopsis of events
since October, 1989, when I came here. Some background
documents are also included, to help you flesh out your
narrative. I would be pleased to write the preface. Please
let me know what you want.

I enjoyed reading your text. It captures the tumultuous
history and the idealistic objectives very nicely. The
College is a virtual symbol of the shifting values in this
country, and our lack of commitment to any long term goals.
Needless to say, I do not know how the drama will end.

Please feel free to call me if you need clarification
on anything.

Sincerely,

Rafael L. Cortada, Ph.D.
President

RLC/jah

Enclosures

COMMUNITY
COLLEGE OF
PHILADELPHIA
1700 Spring Garden Street, Philadelphia, PA 19130

Ronald J. Temple, Ph.D., L.H.D.
President
Telephone: (215) 751-8028

April 29, 1991

Dr. Willie J. Kimmons
Dean
Gaston College
201 Highway 321 South
Dallas, North Carolina 28034-1499

Dear Willie:

I want to apologize for taking such a long time to get this manuscript back to you. As you know, I have only been here ten months, and the pace has been nothing less than phenomenal.

Unfortunately, I have not had the time to develop written comments, although there are many which I would like to make. I think the document could be further enhanced by including more of an analysis of the local and internal difficulties/challenges which Wayne County Community College has faced.

I would include a careful analysis of issues such as: the dominance of unionism as a political force; the political antics of Board members and their failure to grasp the role of boardmanship; political interference of City (Detroit) government, the reasons behind the failure of the college to build sufficient public confidence in order to pass an operating millage; and the reasons and impact of having a succession of presidents, some of whom had no qualifications for the job. These issues I would juxtapose with some of the excellent teaching and scholarship among faculty which is occurring at WCCC and the important contributions the college makes to the county residents as well as to economic development in the region.

Among the accomplishments during my tenure, I would simply list the following:

1. Hiring a senior administrative staff of very competent people;

Letter to Dr. Willie J. Kimmons   -2-

2.   Rebuilding public confidence in the institution as
     documented by a scientific survey commissioned by the
     Michigan State Department of Education;

3.   Restoring full accreditation by the North Central;

4.   Reversing the steep decline in enrollment;

5.   Forging a close partnership with business and industry.

I think you are on the right track with your manuscript. I
hope the above comments are helpful. I would urge you to be more
analytical. I think that would substantially strengthen your
piece. Wayne County Community College is a story waiting to be
told.

Again, please excuse my delay in responding to your
manuscript. Please keep in touch.

Best regards.

                              Sincerely,

                              Ronald J. Temple
                              President

RJT:jtg
Enclosure

COMMUNITY
COLLEGE OF
PHILADELPHIA
1700 Spring Garden Street, Philadelphia, PA 19130-3991

Ronald J. Temple, Ph.D. : Ed.D.
President

January 6, 1992

Dr. Willie Kimmons
Dean, Liberal Arts and Sciences Division
Gaston College
201 Highway 321 South
Dallas, NC 28034-1499

Dear Willie:

I know you must think that I have been negligent because of my lack of response to assist with your document on Wayne County Community College. The pace and the issues in which I am currently involved have not allowed sufficient time for me to work on the document. I anticipate that this condition will continue to at least June, 1992.

I wanted to let you know of my problem so that you can proceed without me. I believe that the project is an important and worthy one, but I will not have the time to give it adequate attention during the next few months. I will be available, however, to discuss any aspect of the project with you by telephone.

Best regards,

Sincerely,

Ronald J. Temple
President

RJT:jdg

April 12, 2007

DR. WILLIE J. KIMMONS

Motivational Speaker

Mrs. Martha J. Grier
Assistant to the Chancellor for Board & Public Relations
Wayne County Community College District
801 W. Fort Street
Detroit, Michigan 48226

Dear Mrs. Grier:

The purpose of this letter is to ascertain pertinent information to include in my book on the history of Wayne County Community College. The title of the book is, The Making of an Urban Community College in a Union and Political Environment: An Historical Perspective of Wayne County Community College, Detroit, Michigan, 1964-2007. The list is as follows:

- A copy of WC3's ten-year annual reports under Dr. Ivery's leadership or any other annual reports or related reports during the College history

- Dr. Ivery's written approval of the Foreword draft I left there in October 2006 for his signature, signed and dated

- WC3's facility plans for the 5 campuses, current and past

- 20 to 30 pictures black and white or color, if you have them of administration buildings, campus buildings, students, staff, faculty, Board of Trustee members, etc.

- Institutional Regional Accreditation reports from SACS

- Any feasibility reports about the College, current and past

"A Voice for
Partners in Education "

1653 Lawrence Circle
Daytona Beach, FL 32117
Office: 386-253-4920
Cell: 386-451-4760
Fax: 386-253-4920
E-mail: WJKimmons@ao .com

- A complete list of Board of Trustee members from the inception of the first board until now with dates they served
- A complete list of all the presidents/chief executive officers of the College with dates they served
- The final chapter of the book will address Dr. Ivery's contributions to the Community College District as the longest serving chief executive officer in WC3's history, October 1995-the present. You and Dr. Ivery may submit information relevant to his leadership accomplishments.

Dr. George Boggs, President of AACC will write the Introduction. I anticipate completing the book by August 2007. Hopefully, I can make a presentation at your October 2007 Professional Development Day Conference and do a book signing of The Making of an Urban Community College in an Union and Political Environment: An Historical Perspective of Wayne County Community College, Detroit, Michigan, 1964-2007.

Mrs. Grier, I want to personally thank you, Dr. Ivery and the WC3 family for your assistance and professional support in this worthwhile project. I am indebted to you, Dr. Ivery and Trustee Juanita Ford.

Sincerely,

Dr. Willie J. Kimmons

83

Willie Kimmons

Subj: **Thank You for Your Call**
Date: 6/2/2009 12.47.49 P.M. Eastern Daylight Time
From: richard.turner@turnerexecutivesearch.com
To: wjkimmons@aol.com

Dr. Kimmons,

It was good to receive your telephone call, this morning, and to learn more about your extensive professional background and activities. Indeed, we have traveled some of the same roads in higher education, e.g., Wayne County Community College District; Bloomington, Indiana. Thanks for bringing me up-to-date, also, regarding several of our mutual friends and colleagues. I visited your impressive Web site, http://savechildrensaveschools.com/home.htm, where I learned more about your life's work.

Please tell me how I may obtain a copy of your book, *The Making of an Urban Community College In a Union and Political Environment: Historical Perspective of Wayne County Community College*, Detroit, Michigan, 1964-2009.

I look forward to further correspondence with you. Best wishes for continued success in your exciting endeavors.

Sincerely,

Richard

Richard M. Turner, III, DME
President Emeritus
Baltimore City Community College, and
Principal
Turner Executive Search Associates, LLC
2000 Town Center, Suite 1900
Southfield, MI 48075
248-353-0557 (Direct)
248-354-1691 (Facsimile)
richard.turner@turnerexecutivesearch.com
http://www.turnerexecutivesearch.com

APPENDIX F

Supporting Articles:

1) WCCC's Events Since October 1, 1990
2) Detroit Free Press, WCCC, Its future depends on Today's plan for reform, November 22, 1990
3) Detroit Free Press, WCCC, Survival is at stake in effort to fix past mistakes, September 19, 1991
4) Detroit Free Press, "New Start" for WCCC, Puts college on change of course, Dr. Rafael Cortada, Former President, WCCC, November 26, 1991
5) Reformer Counts On Survival Atmosphere, Dr. Ronald Temple, Former President, WCCC, July 16, 1986
6) Mr. Claude Chapman, Union leader is sure he's Innocent, Detroit Free Press, March 30, 1992
7) Emerging From The Shadow of Mismanagement, Detroit Free Press, March 30, 1992
8) The Detroit New, Give WCCC to Wayne State, December 18, 1991
9) Yours, College trustee supports millage, Heritage News Herald, March 15, 1992
10) Education and Economic Survival, Dr. Rafael Cortada, Former President, WCCC, March 18-24, 1992
11) Detroit: Now a Ghost Town, Detroit Free Press
12) Woodward Avenue, as seen from The Garfield Building and the Broderick Tower
13) How Detroit Lost Its Way, White Flight, The Honorable Coleman Young, Mayor of Detroit
14) Car Crash, Political Pandering
15) Wayne County Community College District Newsletter, Winter, 2007, District-Wide Celebrating Faculty, Speech by Dr. Willie J. Kimmons, Former President, Downtown Campus, Wayne County Community College (1979-83) on "Closing the Academic Achievement Gap"
16) WCCC District Office

EVENTS SINCE OCTOBER 1, 1990

1. Millage election fails in August 1990- defeat experienced in both Detroit and Wayne County;

2. Dr. Rafael L. Cortada assumes duties as President on October 1, 1990;

3. The 1990-1991 budget, passed by the legislature in July, 1990, continues the special $10.4 million tax grant by one vote. However, the funding bill specifies a phase out of the funding over five (5) years;

4. Analysis indicates that decentralization inflated salaries and staffing. Thus, College has 257 non-teaching staff and 161 faculty for 12,000 students;

5. State audits of enrollment practices and release time procedures from 1985 generate criticism of the College;

6. April, 1991, Board of Trustees passes resolution linking staffing and enrollment. A core staff of 90 is approved for central administration and a core staff of 117 is approved for the five (5) campuses. This reduces management by 50 positions;

7. The Board contracted with Larry Doss for a study of financial and management in July, 1990. The report, issued in November, 1990, reveals serious problems with management, financial controls and accountability. Over 600 recommendations are offered. Board initiates Operation New Start to address problems;

8. April, 1991, Board approves reorganization to centralize reporting. Controls and accountability while reducing staff and maintaining decentralized services based on campuses (Copy enclosed);

9. Board approves specialization for voc tech. programs on each of the campuses;

—2—

10. June, 1991. Legislature approves budget reducing Special
    Tax Grant by one million dollars and scheduling reductions
    of $3.1 million for each of three succeeding years.
    Inasmuch as the tax grant was taken **"off the top"** of
    the community college funding appropriation the other
    28 colleges lobbied against special funding for WCCC;

11. College looks toward 1992 - projected millage election
    (critical), North Central accreditation team visit and
    election for all nine (9) trustees;

12. Dr. Ronald Field, Zoologist from Michigan State and
    Dean, College of Life Sciences at UDC, is appointed
    Vice President for Academic Affairs in June, 1991;

13. Early retirement plan approved by Board in April, 1991,
    enables up to 75 staff to retire. To date, 54 have
    opted to accept.

Detroit Free Press

NOVEMBER 22, 1990

IN OUR OPINION

WCCC
Its future depends on today's plan for reform

Even if Wayne County Community College weren't so important to this region, it should now, once and for all, get its house in order. Because WCCC's future and that of southeastern Michigan and its residents are so inextricably linked, though, the need is more urgent.

The detailed report of an outside consultant — released this week — is a road map for change. Without fundamental change, the college could cease to exist. Its demise would leave a major void and severely limit access to post-secondary education for a large number of Wayne County residents.

During a recent interview with the Free Press editorial board, WCCC President Rafael Cortada — on board only since Oct. 1 — was asked about contingency plans in the event the college loses its special annual subsidy from the state. He responded: "How do you make a contingency plan for losing $10 million?" In commissioning the report, the WCCC Board of Trustees, though, did take the first, tentative step toward planning for a future without state aid.

Years of political infighting, mismanagement

Wayne County Community College

and waste got WCCC into the mess it is now in: internal controls that are "hemorrhaging," information systems that don't produce the information needed to manage college operations effectively, a financial aid program in disarray, a huge amount owed to the college by former students it can't locate. Dr. Cortada and the board, though, won't have nearly so long to clean it up.

Even in the uncertain world of Lansing, the subsidy's eventual elimination is a given. And only the kind of exhaustive reform the report proposes has any chance of persuading Wayne County voters to approve a property-tax levy.

Though bleak in many respects, the picture of the present painted by WCCC's consultant, Larry Doss, a retired accounting firm executive, includes several strengths — among them, certain vocational education programs, a number of successful graduates, and the college's new president.

To that can now be added a strategy — a reasonable, workable strategy — for correcting the deficiencies of the past and helping to ensure the continued availability of the WCCC alternative to coming generations.

14A DETROIT FREE PRESS/THURSDAY, SEPTEMBER 19, 1991

WCCC

Survival is at stake in effort to fix past mistakes

The quiet but deadly serious struggle over the future of Wayne County Community College is at a critical turn. The institution has suffered so many harsh blows that the stakes this time may very well be survival. How well the board supports the administration's efforts to put the school on a sound footing and root out corruption may well determine whether WCCC makes it or not.

What the board must decide now is whether it will confront the use of so-called release time by six faculty members at the school, in a way totally alien to the concept of providing compensation for people diverted from teaching to other duties. The

evidence of double-dipping has been the subject of a major audit. The board chose at its meeting last Friday evening to turn the findings over to prosecutors, to seek the recovery of the money and to evaluate whether to start proceedings aimed at firing, suspending or formally reprimanding the employees, but not to make the report itself public.

Even on the basis of what has already been released, it is clear that the college is facing abuses that have to be dealt with sternly and effectively. The amount of money at stake — $200,000 over three years — is important, but what is more important is that the board must support President Rafael Cortada in his effort to restore integrity to the school.

Wayne County Community College was established without the kind of local millage that is required of most community colleges, and the state has been appropriately pressuring the college to seek local support. What kind of credibility will the college have — either in dealing with the Legislature or with the voters of Wayne County — if it cannot demonstrate that it is operating on an efficient and honest basis?

Dr. Cortada has been taking many of the right steps: reducing the college's overhead, eliminating approximately 50 positions to bring costs down, and fashioning a soundly balanced budget. He has begun to attack the problems of strengthening the educational offerings at the school. What he needs now is for the board to demonstrate the will to support the efforts to impose accountability on the faculty and to root out all possible corruption of the system.

WCCC has the opportunity to overcome the mistakes of its formative years. What must happen now, though, is for the board to be a board and to support what Dr. Cortada must do to correct the mistakes of the past.

Hayden's vision

Martin Hayden, whose life will be celebrated at a memorial service today, was a fierce competitor and a strong force in this community. He shaped his newspaper and his city in accordance with a strong vision and an unyielding sense of values.

Mr. Hayden was also, though, a warm and civil human being — a man who enjoyed telling a good story and exchanging views. He added color and strength to the life of this town and vitality to the Detroit News, over which he presided for so many years.

For us at the Free Press, Martin Hayden may have been the enemy in the Great Newspaper War, but he was also a force with whom we knew we had to reckon. We join with his colleagues and his many friends in honoring him for the role he played in journalism and in Detroit.

Detroit Free Press

Tuesday, Nov. 26, 1991. • Page 3A

'NEW START' FOR WCCC

Cortada puts college on change of course

President focuses on personnel, payroll

By LINDA STEWART
Free Press Staff Writer

Disregard those doomsayers.

Or so says Reinel Cortada, who became president of the embattled Wayne County Community College a year ago.

"Whatever problems the college may have had in the past, the reason it was created as as valid today as it was 25 years ago," Cortada, the school's 10th president, said in a recent interview. "Consequently, it's worth supporting."

Founded in 1967 to provide low-cost education to adults in Wayne County, the school through the years has been plagued by scandals that have sown attention from its union.

But Cortada, with the backing of WCCC's board of trustees, has

launched an aggressive "new start" campaign, including sweeping payroll and personnel revisions, to restore faith in the institution and get it back on an academic track.

"We exist for the benefit of the students, not for the benefit of the administrators or staff," he said. "We want to get our house in order."

So, Cortada is working to bolster the college's academic program, polish its image and make it more fiscally responsible.

But he's got to move fast under trying circumstances. The school is coping with severe budget setbacks — including the phasing out of a $10.4-million annual state subsidy.

With 10,500 students this fall, enrollment is half of what it was 10 years ago. WCCC must grab cash simply trust so voters will approve

a tax increase; the school will seek 1 mill next year to make up for the loss of state money.

The college is also up for re-accreditation next November by the North Central Association of Colleges and Schools, the authority that determines whether changes

Reinel Cortada, president of Wayne County Community College, says he is determined to keep the college afloat and is implementing sweeping changes that affect payroll and personnel. "We want to get our house in order," he said.

MARVIN SHANER
Detroit Free Press

The accrediting team's last visit, in 1987, found the college more stable.

But now the administration is at odds with the faculty union's leadership. While attempting to renegotiate their union ...

In 1984, the association placed WCCC on probation because of problems associated with financial mismanagement, a succession of presidents and nearly four years of political infighting among trustees.

See WCCC, Page 7A

MAR-30-92 MON 11:27 COLLEGE RELATNS   P.08

Cortada puts college
on change of course

WCCC, from Page 3A

ers have not. He has the backing of a cohesive board, state audits are helping direct him, and he's already winning support among the Legislature.

"Cortada walked into a very difficult situation," said state Rep. Joseph Young Sr., D-Detroit, a member of the House subcommittee on community colleges. "But he's begun to do some positive things. He's trying to get a hold of the administration. It seems like the faculty union was running the place. I'm not anti-union, but union can't be management. The managers have to run the college. This is what he's beginning to do."

To help streamline the school's operations and save about $2 million this year, Cortada cut 50 non-teaching staff positions. He also convinced the Legislature not to cut the $10.4 million subsidy all at once.

To prepare current students for jobs of the future, the school is canceling outdated vocational education courses, such as welding, and plans to update or offer a slate of new ones in the next few years.

WCCC also is strengthening its liberal arts and science offerings — making course content and instruction consistent from campus to campus so a student's accumulated credits will transfer smoothly to four-year universities.

"They're improving," Wayne State University admissions director Ron Hughes said of the quality of WCCC graduates, 213 of whom transferred to Wayne State last fall.

In 1982, the college was one of the university's largest suppliers of transfer students. Last year, it ranked in only fourth place because enrollment has dropped significantly in the past decade.

The faculty's dedication is one of the school's strengths, but Cortada offended some instructors with management experience by hiring a handful of outsiders as key administrators to help him centralize operations on WCCC's five campuses. Some faculty members suspect Cortada doesn't trust them. They worry that the administration has brought that mistrust to the bargaining table.

Cortada fiercely denies their suspicions, noting that the state auditor general began investigating WCCC before he arrived.

The state attorney general and the county prosecutor's office are investigating whether members of the faculty union and its bargaining team fraudulently received about $200,000.

"There's no desire to break up the union," Cortada said. "We very much want to have a collective bargaining agreement. But I think every professional is accountable for his or her behavior. . . . It's a question of how public monies were spent."

The investigation focuses on whether some union officials received more pay than they were entitled to.

Claude Chapman, president of the American Federation of Teachers Local 2000, contends that he and the four other faculty members have done nothing wrong. Their contract provisions entitled them to the money they got, he said.

But a preliminary report the state auditor general sent to the college earlier this month tells a different story, according to a copy of WCCC's response, which the Free Press obtained. The report outlines payroll problems at the school between January 1985 and November 1990.

The audit examined three areas: release time and sabbatical leave, sick leave buy-outs and other payroll practices. It reiterates what recent studies commissioned by WCCC have found — abuses were rampant because of lax internal controls.

Cortada and his staff quickly fired back a response to the state that addressed each of the problems. Some of the solutions are as follows:

■ Five employees who were overpaid for release time were asked to return the money. The college has filed a civil suit to recoup the funds.

■ The college is trying to change the procedures that allowed the release time and sabbatical abuses to occur. Some changes are as simple as requiring written proof that a task was performed, and getting a second approval from a vice president before payments are made.

■ To keep employees from being paid when they have unexcused absences, the college has established work schedules and assigned timekeepers to record attendance.

■ Auditors claimed the college's decision to buy out employees' sick leave ended up costing the school more than it saved. So, the college has hired a new controller and director of budget to strengthen its business operations.

■ The entire personnel and payroll office staff has been replaced.

Whatever the state attorney general and county officials find in their investigations, Cortada says, the school must pull together to convince the public it is worthy of the millage it will be seeking next fall.

Rep. Young agrees. "The future of the college depends on whether we can win the confidence of the Wayne County people and pass a millage. That is a must."

Of the 29 community colleges across the state, WCCC is the only one that doesn't levy at least a full mill. The community voted to create the college but declined to approve the taxes to support it. So the Legislature felt obligated to provide the funds. But not anymore.

The Legislature had planned on eliminating WCCC's $10.4-million annual subsidy all at once, but Cortada convinced them to take only $1 million this year and the rest in $3 million increments over the next three years. That, Cortada argued, would give WCCC the chance to improve.

It also would help accomplish another of Cortada's goals: to triple enrollment from 10,300 to 30,900 in the next five years, mainly by advertising and taking care of its students.

"It's a realistic objective," Cortada said. "I think the college is making progress. It has made some significant strides in the past year and has a bright future."

Willie Kimmons

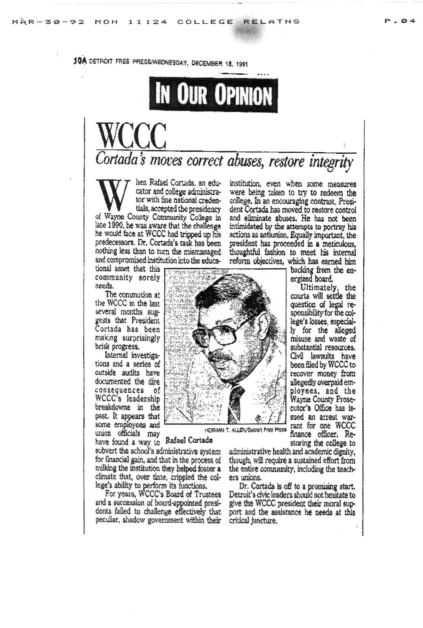

10A DETROIT FREE PRESS/WEDNESDAY, DECEMBER 18, 1991

IN OUR OPINION

WCCC

Cortada's moves correct abuses, restore integrity

When Rafael Cortada, an educator and college administrator with fine national credentials, accepted the presidency of Wayne County Community College in late 1990, he was aware that the challenge he would face at WCCC had tripped up his predecessors. Dr. Cortada's task has been nothing less than to turn the mismanaged and compromised institution into the educational asset that this community sorely needs.

The commotion at the WCCC in the last several months suggests that President Cortada has been making surprisingly brisk progress.

Internal investigations and a series of outside audits have documented the dire consequences of WCCC's leadership breakdowns in the past. It appears that some employees and union officials may have found a way to subvert the school's administrative system for financial gain, and that in the process of milking the institution they helped foster a climate that, over time, crippled the college's ability to perform its functions.

For years, WCCC's Board of Trustees and a succession of board-appointed presidents failed to challenge effectively that peculiar, shadow government within their institution, even when some measures were being taken to try to redeem the college. In an encouraging contrast, President Cortada has moved to restore control and eliminate abuses. He has not been intimidated by the attempts to portray his actions as antiunion. Equally important, the president has proceeded in a meticulous, thoughtful fashion to meet his internal reform objectives, which has earned him backing from the energized board.

Ultimately, the courts will settle the question of legal responsibility for the college's losses, especially for the alleged misuse and waste of substantial resources. Civil lawsuits have been filed by WCCC to recover money from allegedly overpaid employees, and the Wayne County Prosecutor's Office has issued an arrest warrant for one WCCC finance officer. Restoring the college to administrative health and academic dignity, though, will require a sustained effort from the entire community, including the teachers unions.

Dr. Cortada is off to a promising start. Detroit's civic leaders should not hesitate to give the WCCC president their moral support and the assistance he needs at this critical juncture.

HERMAN T. ALLEN/Detroit Free Press
Rafael Cortada

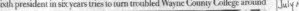

Reformer Counts on 'Survival Atmosphere'

Sixth president in six years tries to turn troubled Wayne County College around July 16, 1986

PHOTOGRAPH FOR THE CHRONICLE BY SUSAN TUSA

Ronald J. Temple, president of Wayne County Community College:
"If we don't pull together now, we'll be torn apart."

By N. SCOTT VANCE

DETROIT

Ronald J. Temple, the reform-minded president of Wayne County Community College here, is counting his blessings as he reflects on his first year in office.

"The possibility was that people could be out in the street, demonstrating, and that the place could have been closed down," he says.

That didn't happen, he adds, in part because there is a "survival atmosphere" on the beleaguered college's five urban campuses. "It's a feeling that what's at stake here is the survival of the institution," he says; "that if we don't pull together now, we'll be torn apart."

Indeed, after years of scandal and administrative upheaval, Mr. Temple's tenure is viewed by many, on the college's campuses and off, as the institution's last chance at redemption.

The college has been rocked in recent years by charges of mismanagement and corruption on the part of its administrators and by fierce political infighting among trustees.

The presidency has changed hands six times since 1980, and the college's travails have provided headline material for Detroit's two newspapers. Partly as a result of the bad publicity, enrollment plummeted from about 23,000 in the late 1970's to under 12,000 this year.

Elected on Reform Platform

In 1984, alarmed state legislators appointed Michigan's Superintendent of Schools to oversee the college. The lawmakers also expanded the board's membership from seven to nine in time for the November 1984 elections. Only three incumbents survived that vote, and the new majority was elected on a reform platform.

Mr. Temple, a specialist in urban history, was the chief executive of the University of Cincinnati's two-year branch, University College, when the new Wayne County board hired him last year. Board members assured him that he would have a free hand to clean house, and he wasted no time in starting.

In his first 10 months in office, he set the stage for a sweeping reorganization of the college's administration and staff, cut and balanced the budget, and gained contract concessions from the faculty union.

In addition, he says he has struggled to change what he calls the "work culture" at the college.

"The work culture had gotten out of hand," says Mr. Temple, who is known for calling staff meetings at 5 p.m. and adjourning them as late as midnight. "Nobody watches the clock now. When I first came in, the deans and chairmen were beating their secretaries out the door at the end of the day."

Such blunt assessments, coupled with his rush to reform, have stirred a furor in some campus quarters. They have also earned him the strong, if tentative, support of legislators, business leaders, and many professors.

"The good thing about Dr. Temple is that for the first time in a long time there is someone at the helm who we have confidence in and who it makes sense to meet halfway," says one professor. "We know that if he fails, we will all fail."

A month after he arrived, Mr. Temple told 44 of the college's top administrators that they would have to compete with candidates from nationwide searches to keep their jobs.

He also persuaded the faculty union to give up most of a scheduled pay raise and to allow Mr. Temple to reassign faculty members, even to non-teaching duties. In return, the 540 full-time and part-time professors received a partial guarantee there would be no layoffs.

Mr. Temple's continued success will hinge largely on his ability to rebuild trust in the college among county residents and state lawmakers, to increase enrollment, and to win cooperation from faculty and staff members.

Stepping Up Recruitment

Mr. Temple has been criticized for paying too much attention to reorganizing the staff and not enough to increasing enrollment. He responds that the college is developing a comprehensive recruitment plan and that he has several strategies to increase enrollment this fall. He is negotiating with Chrysler Corporation to provide courses for as many as 2,000 of their employees under a tuition-benefit program, and he has announced that the college will offer courses in several of Detroit's biggest Baptist churches.

Although many faculty and staff members say they are encouraged by such measures, support for Mr. Temple is far from unanimous.

Among his toughest critics are administrators whose jobs are on the line because of the reorganization. Many have been with the college since its inception in 1969, and they deride the new president for shuffling people into new positions before he knows what their abilities are.

What's more, they complain that they are being overlooked for new assignments simply because they were part of the college's tumultuous past.

"Dr. Temple came in thinking that all of us, to the last person, were grossly incompetent and that nobody was doing a good job," said one administrator who had been at the college for 16 years. "It's true that there have been people who have been incompetent, but there are also many who have done a good job."

Mr. Temple says that he may have overlooked some talented administrators. "There may be some people left in positions now where they have the ability to do more," he says. "I know that's frustrating.

"In the long run, however, the good people will emerge. They will catch fire. I'm a bottom-line type of person. If you can document accomplishment, you'll progress. If you can't, I'll be nice to you, but you won't progress."

Even the professors who like Mr. Temple's results-oriented approach are reluctant to dwell on his initial success. After six presidents in as many years, they're hard to impress.

"It's a hard situation for him," said one professor. "You want to cheer for him, but our voices are hoarse from cheering so many other new presidents in the past."

Union leader is sure he's innocent

School sues over alleged overcharges

BY LINDA STEWART
Free Press Education Writer

Depending on who you talk to, Claude Chapman is either the source of many Wayne County Community College problems or a scapegoat for them.

The state Attorney General's Office and county prosecutor's organized crime task force are investigating whether Chapman, who is president of WCCC's faculty union, took nearly $41,000 in unauthorized pay.

But Chapman is not worried. He is confident that he has done no wrong.

The college claims that Chapman and four other employees frequently were overpaid for certain activities, and in some cases failed to do the work.

For instance, Chapman was released from his duties as a counselor for five hours each week in the winter of 1989 to act as grievance co-chairperson for the union. Apparently, he classified the hours as "instructional overload," which resulted in additional pay. But the college contends he was not entitled to the extra money because he had no teaching obligations.

A law firm hired by the college recently claimed that Chapman and the others developed a release-time and sabbatical scam in which they received $200,000 in salary overpayments over a 3½-year period.

Chapman contends that they have never received any money that they were not entitled to under the provisions of their faculty contract. He says the contract is being misinterpreted by their accusers.

"It was designed to have this flexibility," said Chapman, who joined the college's staff in 1972. "Any review will show that's true."

Although a few faculty members have long been suspicious of Chapman's financial dealings, the majority are behind him. They feel gratitude for everything good they have in the way

of salary and benefits.

"Claude is the most understanding person I've ever known in terms of not bearing grudges," said biology teacher Morris Dunbar. "We've had labor peace since they've been in office."

It's a strong union, one that has secured well-paying contracts for its 460 full- and part-time members of the American Federation of Teachers Local 2000. But recently they've run into some trouble.

The faculty is working under the terms of a contract that expired August 31. To negotiate a new one, they've gone to mediation.

Last year, Chapman was the second highest paid person on WCCC's payroll, having earned nearly $88,000. The union's chief negotiator, Thomas (Tony) Randolph, was right behind him with $78,418. Only the college president earned more — about $97,000.

While many might argue that union leaders should be well-compensated, the administration contends that the bulk of their salaries were obtained fraudulently.

WCCC filed a civil suit against Chapman and Randolph last month, alleging that they duped the college. The suit filed in Wayne County Circuit Court claims Chapman was overpaid $40,861 from the winter of 1988 through the spring of 1990.

> ## "According to the contract, I can go to the moon or law school or the jungle. There's nothing wrong with me doing that, it's legal."
>
> Thomas Randolph,
> faculty negotiator accused of receiving illegal compensation

The school claims Randolph owes $39,047 for "illegal compensation" he received from 1986 through 1990, the bulk of which he was paid while on a year's sabbatical in 1987. The college contends that Randolph went to law school instead of doing a required research project during his sabbatical. Randolph said he completed the project and has the research report to prove it.

"These charges are unfair and baseless," Randolph said. "According

to the contract, I can go to the moon or law school or the jungle. There's nothing wrong with me doing that, it's legal."

WCCC demanded repayment April 23 and Sept. 17, but Chapman and Randolph refused.

The duo suspect the latest allegations are political, noting that the board of trustees has always ratified the contract provisions for their salaries in the past and the state has not cited it as a problem in earlier audits.

"It's my guess that they think if they can run Claude and I out of there, they can handle everyone else," Randolph said. "This stuff about release time is a bogus issue."

The state auditor general has conducted its own investigation, and a final report is expected sometime in December.

Whatever the findings, Chapman, who is not up for re-election until 1994, stressed that he works hard for his money and has served the union well during his 16-year tenure. Each time he has run for office, he has been unopposed.

He said he has no intention of "moving aside."

But, Chapman added, if the school wants to drop the lawsuit and work out some sort of early retirement package, he might be willing to listen.

Claude Chapman, president of Wayne County Community College's faculty union, is accused of taking nearly $41,000 in unauthorized pay. Chapman, who joined WCCC in 1972, insists he has done no wrong.

WILLIAM ARCHIE/Detroit Free Press

EMERGING FROM THE SHADOW OF MISMANAGEMENT

"If Wayne County doesn't get its population up, we'll have a revolution in this town.... We won't have a skilled labor force.... Without an educated citizenry, this town will blow up."

The Rev. Charles Morton, WCCC board chairman

Wayne County Community College makes higher education available to low-income people. But for years the college has operated under a shadow of financial mismanagement and incompetence. Last year, its nine-member board of trustees appointed Rafael Cortada, PhD, as president and ordered him to clean up the mess. But time and money are running out.

■ Background: WCCC is a public two-year institution that offers occupational/career programs in addition to traditional liberal arts courses that can transfer to universities. Despite its problems, the college has a highly regarded urban teachers program, natural resources program, and nursing training.

Founded in 1967, the college opened its doors two years later and now has programs on five campuses in Detroit, Belleville and Taylor.

■ Enrollment: 10,300 students this fall. Ten years ago it was 20,325.

■ Tuition: $37 per credit hour, one of the lowest in the Detroit area.

■ Operating budget: $36 million.

■ Operating budget comes from local taxes, tuition and state appropriations. This fall, the college was hit with a $4 million cut in state appropriations and a $1 million cut in a state subsidy.

Compiled by Free Press Education Writer Linda Stewart

10A THE DETROIT NEWS WEDNESDAY, DECEMBER 18, 1991

The Detroit News

Give WCCC to Wayne State

A new state audit has all but dashed any chance that county residents will approve an operating millage for Wayne County Community College (WCCC). For the second time this year, Auditor General Thomas H. McTavish found that WCCC misspent or misappropriated millions of dollars. Taxpayers and students might be better served if WCCC were absorbed by Wayne State University.

The audit, which covered the period from January 1985 through November 1990, revealed that paychecks were issued to people who could not be verified as employees. Some $2.3 million was used to buy out unused sick leave, with numerous employees receiving double their entitlement.

Auditors found little evidence that some workers actually earned their salaries. In one instance, auditors said there was no proof that a one-time counselor and president of the WCCC Federation of Teachers "performed productive and meaningful work on behalf of the college" in exchange for his $81,395 salary. Another worker, who reportedly helped students qualify for government aid from her home, could not remember the name of any of the students she assisted. Others were allowed to take paid time off without accounting for how it was spent.

This was only the latest in a series of allegations about corruption, mismanagement, nepotism and unqualified instructors since WCCC's opening in 1967. In March, an audit found that some WCCC instructors submitted phony student enrollments to pad their paychecks. Last year, a state audit charged that college officials misused $24 million for building and improvement funds.

In 1984, the state Legislature forced an overhaul of WCCC operations and the college was placed on academic probation. At least four of 10 presidents have been forced out of office.

The latest WCCC president, Rafael Cortada, took over in October, so it's not fair to blame him for the outrages. Indeed, Mr. Cortada has eliminated 50 nonteaching positions and installed new financial controls. The college ended last year with a budget surplus.

But it seems clear that Mr. Cortada is operating with a rotten structure. The problems may be too entrenched to be resolved without a thorough-going change. Folding WCCC into WSU would be a logical step. The precedent has already been established by the University of Cincinnati, which runs the area's community college system.

Such an approach would allow elimination of overlap and better oversight of both finances and curriculum. It would also make it easier for successful two-year students to transfer into a senior college program.

WCCC's checkered history dispels hope that public confidence in a free-standing WCCC will ever be sufficient to earn voter support for a millage. Last August, voters rejected a 1-mill property tax levy to replace $14.5 million in state subsidies being phased out by the Legislature. The only solution is to fold WCCC into a respected institution like WSU — or close it altogether.

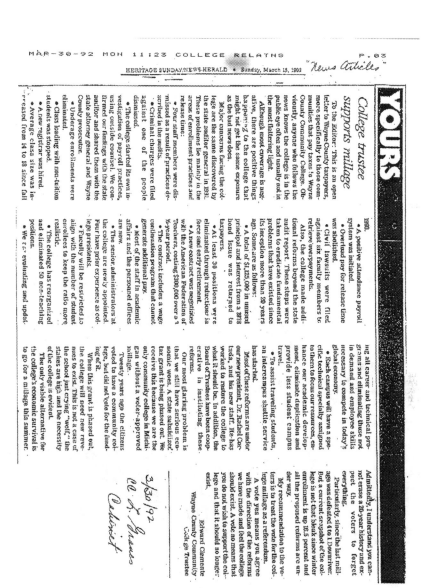

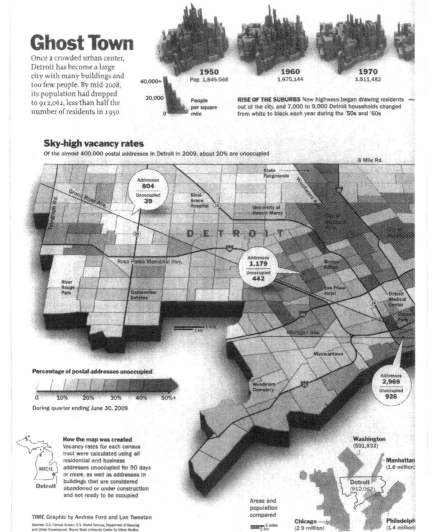

Ghost Town

Once a crowded urban center, Detroit has become a large city with many buildings and too few people. By mid-2008, its population had dropped to 912,062, less than half the number of residents in 1950

1950 Pop. 1,849,568

1960 1,670,144

1970 1,511,482

40,000+
20,000
0

People per square mile

RISE OF THE SUBURBS New highways began drawing residents out of the city, and 7,000 to 9,000 Detroit households changed from white to black each year during the '50s and '60s

Sky-high vacancy rates

Of the almost 400,000 postal addresses in Detroit in 2009, about 20% are unoccupied

Addresses
804
Unoccupied
39

Addresses
1,179
Unoccupied
442

Addresses
2,969
Unoccupied
926

Percentage of postal addresses unoccupied

0   10%   20%   30%   40%   50%+

During quarter ending June 30, 2009

How the map was created
Vacancy rates for each census tract were calculated using all residential and business addresses unoccupied for 90 days or more, as well as addresses in buildings that are considered abandoned or under construction and not ready to be occupied

MICH.
Detroit

TIME Graphic by Andréa Ford and Lon Tweeten

Sources: U.S. Census Bureau; U.S. Postal Service; Department of Housing and Urban Development; Wayne State University Center for Urban Studies

Areas and population compared

5 miles
5 km

Washington
(591,833)

Manhattan
(1.6 million)

Detroit
(912,062)

Chicago
(2.9 million)

Philadelphia
(1.4 million)

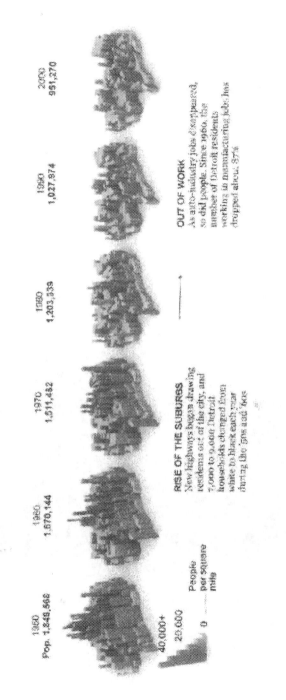

Detroit: Now a Ghost Town

1950
Pop. 1,849,568

1960
1,670,144

1970
1,511,482

1980
1,203,339

1990
1,027,974

2000
951,270

People
per square
mile

40,000+

20,000

0

RISE OF THE SUBURBS
New highways began drawing residents out of the city, and 7,000 to a year. Detroit households changed from white to black each year during the '50s and '60s.

OUT OF WORK
As auto-industry jobs disappeared, so did people. Since 1960, the number of Detroit residents working in manufacturing jobs has dropped about 37%.

Picture printed with permission Yves Marchand

Woodward Avenue is the main street around which the downtown and the rest of the city developed.
Many buildings along Woodward Avenue remain abandoned, despite the gradual gentrification of the
town center.
WOODWARD AVENUE SEEN FROM THE BRODERICK TOWER
IN THE EARLY DAYS THE WAYNE COUNTY COMMUNITY COLLEGE ORIGINAL CENTRAL OFFICES AND
SOME CLASSROOMS WERE ON 8904 WOODWARD AVENUE WHICH IS NOW CLOSED.

How Detroit Lost Its Way

White flight
Latent racial tensions exploded into rioting in July 1967, killing 43 people and sending thousands of white Detroiters to the suburbs. The exodus institutionalized racial divisions that have only hardened since

Coleman Young
Suburbanization turned Detroit into a majority-African-American city, and its first black mayor spent his 20-year tenure playing the politics of retribution

Car crash
Union leaders tailored their policies to suit the mighty auto industry, whose leaders ignored the growing threat from abroad. When the carmakers stalled, Detroit was left without a diverse industrial base

Political pandering
In an effort to prop up their constituencies, politicians like Representative John D. Dingell resisted sensible policies, like more-stringent mileage standards, that would have helped Detroit compete today

Desolation row
An example of the city's decay, the Lee Plaza Hotel ballroom lies vacant

How Detroit Lost Its Way
White Flight

Latent racial tensions exploded into rioting in July 1967, killing 43 people and sending thousands of white Detroiters to the suburbs. The exodus institutionalized racial divisions that have only hardened since

Coleman Young

Suburbanization turned Detroit into a majority-African-American city, and its first black mayor spent his 20-year tenure playing the politics of retribution

Car Crash

Getty
Car Crash

Union leaders tailored their policies to suit the mighty auto industry, whose leaders ignored the growing threat from abroad. When the carmakers stalled, Detroit was left without a diverse industrial base

Political Pandering

Getty
Political pandering

In an effort to prop up their constituencies, politicians like Representative John D. Dingell resisted sensible policies, like more-stringent mileage standards, that would have helped Detroit compete today

Wayne County Community College District Newsletter Winter 2007 District-Wide Celebrating Faculty, Speech by Dr. Willie J Kimmons former President Downtown Campus Wayne County Community College (1979-83) on "Closing the Academic Achievement Gap" pg. 12

SPECIAL FEATURE

District-Wide
CELEBRATING FACULTY

SPECIAL INTEREST SESSIONS

1. Adjusting to changing Circumstances to Encourage Student Success – Kinda Zara Herbert, Wayne State University Department or Interdisciplinary Studies

2. What's New in Payroll and Human Resources at WCCCD – Gail Arnold and Anna Reteach G

3. Administering Learning Communities with Focus on the Urban Institution – Victoria Tarke, Ph. D, Distinguished University Professor Systemic University and Clinic of Higher Education Program.

4. Postmodern Pedagogy: Teaching and Learning with Generation Next – Mark Taylor, M. S. W., B.L 13, USO Taylortrogram.org

5. "The Art of Giving Great Service" Zingerman's Zing Train – East Yelvo and Ann MacDougald, Consultants, Zingerman's Training Inc.

6. Using Voice Tools to Increase Interaction and Student Engagement – Dr. Lenore Likens and Mark Romeo II, Wimba Representative

7. Closing the Academic Achievement Gap – Dr. Willie Kimmons, Author and Motivational Speaker

8. Information Session UAW and PAAA, Denny Norris and Mary OS

9. CVS Customer Service Testing

10. The Net Works – Glenda Snyder, QSO, Student Counseling

WCCC District Office.

Printed in the United States
By Bookmasters